His Praise Goes On

Kay D. Rizzo

His Praise

Goes On

REVIEW AND HERALD® PUBLISHING ASSOCIATION
HAGERSTOWN, MD 21740

The author assumes full responsibility for the accuracy of all facts
and quotations as cited in this book.

This book was
Edited by Gerald Wheeler
Copyedited by Jocelyn Fay and James Cavil
Designed by Kimberly Haupt
Cover photos by PhotoDisc
Typeset: 13/16 Berkeley

PRINTED IN U.S.A.

05 04 03 02 01   5 4 3 2 1

R&H Cataloging Service
Rizzo, Kay Darlene, 1943-
    His praise goes on: thanking God from a full heart.

    1. Christian life.   2. Religious life.   3. Worship.   I. Title.

        248.4

ISBN 0-8280-1433-7

Dedication

To Francis De Lillo,
for your loving and continued support.

Contents

His Praise Goes On

"I'm thanking you, God, from a full heart, I'm writing the book on your wonders. I'm whistling, laughing, and jumping for joy; I'm singing your song, High God."
—Psalm 9:1, 2, Message

"Thanking God from a full heart?" Today my heart is full. In the next room rests a delightfully healthy baby, Jarod, my first grandchild. He entered our lives on November 30, 1997, and nothing has been the same since. The child turns our nights into days and fills our days with laughter. Of course, he's the most beautiful, most talented, and most advanced child to be born in this century. Well, so I exaggerate a little. Isn't that what new grandmas are supposed to do? Regardless, my heart overflows with gratitude and praise for my Father. But even before Jarod came to bless our lives, my heart was full of joy. For you see, my heavenly Father has a way of keeping my heart brimming with blessings regardless of circumstances.

While I'm not sure if the number of my blessings has increased since I began praising, it seems it has. For I see His gentle handiwork everywhere I look in my life and in those of others. Then again, perhaps God has only opened my eyes so I can see and appreciate the blessings He's been sending my way all along. Through praise, I've caught a glimpse of His reality instead of mine.

John wrote in the book of Revelation that in the latter days God's people would have poor vision—a spiritual myopia or nearsightedness. We'd focus on ourselves. In order to see God's reality, we would need heavenly eyesalve. The curative eyesalve John described is available to the woman who sings God's praises and to the man who glorifies His name. It is waiting for me!

When I apply this divine medication, blinding scales fall off my eyes. I can see the blessings visible to my five senses, and beyond that to the greater blessings that are intangible to my physical senses. I love it. I can walk through a grocery store or drive down the highway invincible to life's irritations—a selfish driver, a shopping cart collision, a red light at the wrong time.

Instead of being frustrated at the inconvenience and losing my cool, I sense God's presence. God replaces my worried frown with a secret little smile, for I can, with the wonder of a child, see God's handiwork everywhere.

It's as if my world comes alive every morning. I see the mysteries of a dandelion for the first time all over again and praise my Creator. As I feel a gentle breeze it reminds that the Holy Spirit is quietly working in my heart. I hear God's voice speaking to me through the song of the mockingbird and the robin. Joy wells up inside of me, spilling out onto others. And like the psalmist, I'm writing this book about His wonders.

I whistle, sing, laugh, and jump for joy! Before I found the joy in God's salvation; before I discovered the kingdom of God to be mine in the here and now; before I came across the power in praising, not regardless of my circumstances, but because I can know God is working through my circumstances—my heart was dead. A world of brutality and careless indifference had murdered it.

I couldn't sing or whistle. Nor could I laugh or feel joy. The truth is that while I still can't whistle, I certainly sing a bunch and laugh a lot, and Nike or Reebok can't make athletic shoes that can duplicate the abundant spring God has placed in my step.

Anything less is counterfeit and not worth my time.

Praise is the purest form of worship, not a religious game we play with the King of the universe. Praising is not a magic formula for success in life. Nor is it a new way of praying in order to manipulate God. Rather, it is a way of life solidly backed by God's Word. I praise God not for what I can get from Him, but for who He is. Should I choose to praise God for what I can get, nothing would happen. My praise would be phony.

A preacher meeting Gabriel at the pearly gates expected to walk right into the kingdom. Instead, Gabriel shook his head sadly. "I'm sorry, but your name isn't on my list."

"What?" The minister was indignant. "How can that be? There must be some mistake. I preached the Word of God faithfully for more than 50 years!"

"H'mmm." Gabriel thought for a moment. "That should earn you 10 points."

"Ten points? How many points do I need to get in?"

"Two thousand."

"And 50 years as a minister is worth only 10 points? Does it help if I didn't have an assistant for most of those years?"

Gabriel shrugged. "OK, 12 points."

"What do I do now?"

The angel glanced away from the kingdom toward a frighteningly dark hole in the stratosphere below.

"No! I don't belong there!" the preacher gasped. "Certainly if I list all the good things I did over the years they'll add up to 2,000. That's it! I'll make a list."

He reached into his briefcase and hauled out a laptop computer. "H'mmm, let's see . . ." His fingers rested for a second on the keys, then he began typing furiously. Finally confident that he'd listed enough good deeds to qualify for entrance, he handed the laptop to Gabriel.

The angel squinted at the screen, mumbling as he read, "Pastor for 50-plus years—12 points. Baptized thousands—

seven points. Volunteered at the local soup kitchen one day a week for 10 years—two points."

"Two points?" The pastor gasped.

Gabriel continued. "Cared for four foster children—four points. Served on the mission board—one point. Took missionary junket to Africa in the summer of 1974—one point. Straight A's in college." Gabriel glanced over the computer screen at the preacher. The minister's face reddened as he cleared his throat.

"Except for Greek—an A–."

Gabriel deleted the preacher's reference to college from the screen and continued. "Donated clothes to Goodwill—one point. Helped relocate family with four children after house fire—three points. Rescued a kitten from a tree?" This time Gabriel arched his eyebrows.

The preacher shrugged. "I was getting desperate."

"Shared your fire truck with your little brother?"

The man shrugged. "What can I say?"

"H'mmm." Gabriel began tabulating the points the man had acquired. "Twelve, 19, 21 . . ."

All the while Gabriel was questioning the preacher at the pearly gates other people were streaming into the city with barely more than a wave and a smile at the archangel. So it was with reluctance that Gabriel gave the preacher the bad news. Frustrated, the preacher exploded, "I don't understand it! I lived my whole life dedicated to serving God. I deserve better."

At that moment a group of teenagers sauntered up to the gates and greeted Gabriel with hugs and smiles. And, as he had with the others, the angel let them into the city.

"What's going on here?" the preacher complained. "The entire time I've been here making my list of good deeds, people have been marching through the gates. Why don't they have to make out lists?"

Gabriel turned toward the preacher. "Sir, they're not playing the game."

Ouch! What a punch line. It hits many Christians right where they live. When my pastor shared the preacher's tale with us during his sermon, I missed the rest of what he had to say, the story made such an impression.

Like the preacher, I've played at the game of salvation. Having set my heart on the prize, I determined to get to heaven any way I could. And like the preacher, I discovered I can never feed enough of the world's hungry, never give enough hours of service, or sing enough hymns to earn the right to eternal life. It wasn't until I threw away my scorecard, my bonus points, and my spinner for the Going to Heaven game that I could find the assurance of the kingdom and eternal life. No games, no gimmicks, no joke—just eternal life in Jesus.

Recently a similar story came over the Internet. The punch line had the frustrated pastor exclaim to Gabriel, "How can anyone earn heaven, but for the grace of God!"

Then Gabriel smiles and says, "You finally figured it out. Welcome home."

Whichever story you prefer, the lesson is clear—it will always take God's grace to get there. There's no stair step of righteousness that you or I can climb during our lifetimes, leaving the gap between us and salvation for Jesus' grace to fill. If that were so, some would be able to boast that they'd climbed more steps than their neighbor and that it took less grace to save them than it did to save someone else. The amount of grace, the price of salvation, is the same for each of us—the sacrifice of Jesus Christ. For this I can praise my Father. And for this I praise the Son.

The abbreviations A.D. (anno Domini, or "the year of our Lord") and B.C. (before Christ) divide historical time. In a similar manner, I measure my spiritual life with A.P. (after I discovered praise) and B.P. (before I discovered praise). That's how much my life has changed since the Lord unleashed the powerhouse of praise within me. I've learned that praise and prayer make a potent spiritual cocktail. Best of all, I've discovered that praising is the key to letting God get on with His work in me. It allows me to get out of His way.

In B.P. time I played those spiritual games just as the preacher in the story. I hoped to gain access to God, not as a search for the being of God, but as a way to manipulate Him for my own purposes.

In a series of television ads a man sidled up to a friend and said, "I love you, man." His motive was to con his friend into sharing the advertised product. It didn't work for the character in the commercial, and it won't work for us with God either. If the purpose for praising is to con God out of a few goodies, I'll be disappointed. My spiritual thirst will never be quenched, nor my self-serving wants satisfied.

Instead of asking "What can You do for me, God?" praise teaches me to ask "What's next, Father? Where do we go from here?" And instead of playing Going to Heaven like the preacher in the story, my God and I have set off for a fabulous adventure on the wings of praise.

During the past few years we've soared like eagles above events in my life that should have sent me crashing to the rocks below. He's led me to the source of incredible riches, to a wealth that never runs out.

Ten years ago, if I could have viewed my life today, I would have been speechless with awe. My Father in heaven had so many surprises in store for me that my imagination wouldn't have been able to grasp it. He's carried me on His wings to "far-away places with strange sounding names." (As I write this, I am sitting in the Los Angeles Airport awaiting a flight to Tortola, British West Indies. Who would have thought that possible? Who could have imagined what God had in store for me?)

As a child I read great books about the search for the Holy Grail, for the Lost Dutchman's Mine in Arizona's Superstition Mountains, and of Coronado's quest for the Seven Cities of Cibola. Such adventure stories of courage and determination never failed to captivate and stimulate my imagination. And they still do.

Once I read a book about some children living in Florida who uncovered a pirate's treasure chest in their grandfather's backyard. While I knew few pirates ever sailed as far north as New York State to bury their treasures, I reasoned that since two wars had been fought in the Hudson River valley—the French and Indian War and the American Revolution—maybe someone, while trying to escape a pursuing enemy, took the time to bury a treasure chest of gold in my backyard. The person would have planned to return for it, but alas, did not survive to do so. It could happen, right?

Convinced my logic was feasible, I took a shovel from our garage, chose a spot toward the center of our lot, and started digging. I dug all morning and well into the afternoon. Then, after drinking gallons of water, I dug some more. Somewhere along the way I shed my jacket and dirtied my face and clothes. When my best friend, Patty Brown, came over to play, I let her in on my secret. She agreed to dig for a while too.

We were making great progress when my mother called to me to come inside for the night. Dropping the shovel, I ran to obey. I'd barely washed the grime from my hands, face, and arms when I heard an angry cry of pain. In the dark my father had stepped into the hole I'd dug.

My search for buried treasure stopped abruptly. The next morning I refilled the hole and returned the shovel to the garage. So as far as I know, the early American treasure hidden in the backyard of my childhood home is still there, if anyone is interested in continuing my search.

When I began my adventure of praise, I had no idea the extent of the treasures I would uncover as I dug into God's Word. I couldn't imagine the exciting twists and turns my life would take. Nor could I see the number of valleys of the shadow of death my God and I would pass through or the mountaintops we'd claim in the name of Jesus Christ. And tomorrow's adventures? I can only wonder and eagerly ask, "What's next, Father?"

Setting My Focus

"Every day I will praise you and extol your name for ever and ever."
—*Psalm 145:2*

My choice today is to praise my God. He already knows the day's outcome, and He holds both my day and me securely in His hands. Therefore I can praise the outcome as it unfolds before me. My attention will remain focused on my heavenly Father and not on my changing circumstances.

The psalmist vowed to praise God every day with no "Perhaps" or "Maybe" or "If the weather's good." He declared that he would maintain his focus on the Father with his praise. Regardless of the outside pressures, despite the inner insecurities, David said, "I rejoice in the Lord" (Ps. 104:34).

I'm not much of a photographer. For many years part of my problem was in focusing the lens. My eyeglasses kept getting in the way. When the automatic focus cameras came along and did the focusing for me, I rejoiced. Thanks to technology all I had to do was point and shoot—a great improvement. I love the newer video cameras with the miniature TV screen on the side so I can see exactly what it is I'm photographing at all times. No more peepholes for my glasses to click against. And no more having to adjust the lens while my beautiful Kodak moment evaporates.

For many of the same reasons I am not much of a birdwatcher either. When bird-watching, I not only need to focus the lens of the binoculars on my feathered friend—when I can see him at all in the foliage—but have to focus my mind on the reason I've chosen to sit on the edge of a swamp at such an unearthly hour in the first place! No wonder I have trouble seeing the beauty of a blue-bellied, ruby-throated chickadee when my focus centers on the mosquitoes biting my arms and the disease-infected ticks dangling from my trouser legs.

Don't misunderstand me. I love birds. I can understand why Satan might want to exterminate them from our planet. Nothing can speak to me of God's goodness and love more clearly than the cheerful praise coming from the throat of one of God's songbirds.

My mother loved birds. She had a unique talent of imitating a bird's song so well that she could fool the bird. She would lure a bird almost within touching distance. So I do appreciate the creatures.

Maybe if my vision were better, maybe if all those blood-sucking, disease-carrying creatures weren't lurking in the grass to nip, bite, and torment me—maybe then I'd enjoy bird-watching. And maybe then I could stay focused on my purpose for being out there in the wilderness.

Sound familiar? "I'd be a happy Christian if . . ." The excuses are as flimsy as are mine regarding bird-watching. "If only my troubles would go away, I could rejoice and give God the glory." Or "If I hadn't been the victim of abuse as a child . . ." "If my husband didn't drink so much . . ." "If my children were more obedient . . ." "If I weren't too busy scratching out a living to focus on the goodness of God . . ." Our lists of excuses are endless!

It's all in the focus. When we lived in Oregon my family and I took numerous journeys to the coast. Wise parents never forget two rules while on the Oregon beach with their children: never turn your back on your children, and never turn your back on the surf.

One day I did both. I was building a sand castle while my husband, Richard, took our daughters, Rhonda and Kelli, to visit the lighthouse on the cliffs above the beach. Intent on finishing the details of my masterpiece, I paid little notice when daughter number one returned.

I mumbled my thanks when she admired my sand castle, but failed to notice that she had wandered over to the water's edge, just beyond my view. I heard her call, "Mama, there's a Japanese glass float!"

Japanese glass floats were becoming more and more rare on the Oregon coast, so I should have been alerted to her next move. The next sound I heard was a sharp cry. I glanced up in time to see Rhonda's head bobbing in the surf. Screaming, I leaped to my feet and dashed into the water after my child. Rhonda disappeared behind a huge wave. Adrenaline pumped through my body as I bounded toward her. She surfaced again farther from shore.

As I fought against the waves, Richard shot past me in a blur. He grabbed Rhonda just before a wave pulled her under the surface of the water. They bobbed to the surface, my husband clutching Rhonda and Rhonda hanging on to the float. Richard fought the waves with superhuman strength while I continued out to meet him. Kelli stood on the beach, looking terrified and bewildered.

It seemed like an eternity before my husband thrust my child into my arms, then collapsed on the sand. Relieved, I clung to Rhonda until she begged me to release her. We held an impromptu praise service. As a postscript to the story, Rhonda had risked her life not for a rare Japanese float, but for a plastic Norwegian one, cracked at that!

Nothing on earth was so important to me as my family. Not financial portfolios, not cars or clothes or employment, and certainly not houses or lands. Yet I'd lost my focus over the trivial. I'd been so busy building my sand castle that I'd forgotten to stay alert to the dangers of the surf and to its threat to my daughter. Easy for parents to do, isn't it? Being so busy building castles of sand that we forget the more important elements of life.

A young mother agonizes over the cellulite on her thighs, forgetting that she should be enjoying her three small children, not obsessing over her bodily imperfections. A father spends more time chatting on the Internet than with his teenage son. A daughter scolds and belittles her aging mother, not realizing how much she'll miss those last days together. Focus—it's all in the focus.

Marathon runner Frank Shorter boarded a jet for Munich, Germany, the city of his birth. A member of the United States running team, Frank would compete against his native countrymen in the 1972 Olympics. Making the team had been a lifelong dream. And the fact that he'd get to visit Germany in the process added to his joy.

Frank toured the city, taking in the sights he'd heard about from his parents. The upcoming race limited his sightseeing, though. Despite his enthusiasm at visiting Germany, he didn't want to lose sight of his purpose for being there.

On the day of the 26-mile race all thoughts other than of winning left his mind. Step by step, lob by lob, he ran. During the first nine miles he maintained a good rhythm. Bored with the slow pace, Frank accelerated, slowly pulling ahead of the pack. He maintained the first position throughout the rest of the race.

As Frank entered the stadium at the end of the course, he expected to be greeted with cheers and applause. Instead, he emerged from the tunnel onto the track to a deafening roar of booing and whistling. Confused, he wondered what he'd done wrong. Yet he continued running in spite of the audience's negative reception.

What Frank didn't know was that minutes before he'd arrived in the stadium, a spectator had leaped from the stands and run a full lap around the track before security guards caught him and hauled him away. The shouts of censure were aimed at the errant spectator, not Frank.

From Frank's point of view the boos seemed aimed at him. No one else was around, or so he thought. It would have been tempting for Frank, after receiving such a terrible reception, to quit. But he didn't. Frank Shorter ignored the seeming censure, completed the race, and won the gold medal for the United States.

During those long days of training, Frank learned a valuable lesson, one that would make the difference between failure and victory. He learned the secret of Philippians 3:13, 14: "Forgetting what is behind . . . I press on toward the goal." By blocking out all distractions and focusing on his goal, he would cross the finish line and win the gold.

A story from World War II tells of a pig that wandered between the warring forces. Instead of shelling the enemy, the U.S. troops began taking potshots at the pig. The GI's lost the battle, not because superior forces overwhelmed them, but because they lost their focus.

Losing one's focus will defeat you every time. Hebrews 12:2 warns: "Let us fix our eyes on Jesus." It's so simple to maintain your focus when the crowd is cheering you on, when friends and family shout words of encouragement from the bleachers, when the birds sing and the sun shines. But when the storm clouds roll in, when the spectators boo and hiss, that's when your focus really matters.

At one of the many points in my life when my spirits sagged and I was ready to throw in the proverbial towel, a wise friend, who'd been through his own storms, said, "Kay, remember the circus wagons of olden times. When they'd roll into town, the little dogs would bark and bite at the wheels, creating a terrible ruckus. But the circus wagons ignored the dogs and just kept rolling on." It was a different way of saying to maintain one's focus.

Whenever trouble brews, I must choose whether to give up

or keep my focus. Will I throw in the towel or use it to gird up my loins? When I've done my best only to have people criticize my efforts, when I'm misinterpreted and feel tempted to pick up my marbles and walk away, it's my choice.

My adventure of praise is a marathon, not a sprint. I will praise my Father not only on sunny days but in the midst of the deluge. That's my choice. But the only way I can maintain the pace of this rugged adventure called life and not collapse in a pothole along the way is by keeping my focus on Jesus Christ through my "sacrifice of praise" (Heb. 13:15). No stray pigs, yapping dogs, or booing spectators can divert my attention from my purpose to glorify my Saviour—unless I choose to let them.

Two

Joy in a World Gone Mad

"Those who trust in the Lord are like Mount Zion, which cannot be shaken but endures forever."
—Psalm 125:1

I don't understand it. It just doesn't make sense!" Have you ever said that? Perhaps you uttered those phrases over a marriage breakup or a child running away from home. If you're hoping the things of our world will make sense to you, don't bet your retirement account on it. How can anyone make sense out of a world gone mad?

Take grass, for instance—not marijuana, just common everyday lawn grass. Have you ever noticed how well it grows in your flower garden, but how much it has to struggle to take root in the area you've designated as your lawn? I don't understand it.

Or consider the weekly wash. Before you take the last load of wash from the dryer, clothes have already begun to pile up for the next washday.

Or if we can measure the speed of light, why can't we measure the speed of dark? Why do they place braille signs at drive-up ATMs? If there are disgruntled employees, how come you never hear about gruntled employees? What's another word for synonym? Why isn't there mouse-flavored cat food? And why does Hawaii have interstate highways?

Life is full of questions, many of them without easy answers.

Some of life's questions, like the ones above, are nonsense. Many other questions that aren't so humorous spring from aching hearts and troubled souls. Why did my dad die of cancer? Why did I lose three babies? Why must my friend Judy suffer from MS? Why, Lord, why?

To say that praise answers such questions would be a cruel lie. Praise isn't the answer. Faith is. "And we know that all things work together for good to those who love God, to those who are the called according to His purpose" (Rom. 8:28, NKJV).

God said it, and His children accept it as gospel truth. That's called faith. But faith alone has no voice. It's a silent thing that grows inside us only as we exercise it. Is there virtue to suffering in silence? Perhaps, but for suffering to glorify God, we must give it voice—not the suffering itself, but the faith that grows from it. That's where praise comes in. Praise gives voice to the faith nurtured within us. And there exists no more fragrant perfume to the Father than the aroma of praise watered with our tears. "They that sow in tears shall reap in joy" (Ps. 126:5, KJV).

Praise is to faith what exercise is to the muscles of the body. According to the weather, I have two exercise routines. On good days I walk for 30 minutes and swim for 40 minutes each day. And when the weather's bad, I resort to my stationary bike. Some days the last thing I want to do is exercise, no matter how good I know I'll feel once I get started or how great it is for my aging heart. Once I drag myself off my water bed, tie on my walking shoes, and stumble out the door, it gets easier, right? Wrong. At times even after I finish walking, count off the last rotation on the Exercycle, or swim the last lap I still wish I could close the blinds and pull the bedcovers up over my head.

Yet I can be confident that the exercise is doing its thing on my heart and muscles regardless of how I feel or even look. Praise, the exercise of faith, doesn't take as much time to produce visible rewards. When I bring the "sacrifice of praise" (Heb. 13:15) to the Lord, my words may begin as stiff and unnatural as the movements of a mechanical windup toy, but if I persist in praising, before I know it the Holy Spirit seeps into the hidden recesses of my mind and takes control of my emotions. My words act on my mind, causing the corners of my lips constantly to bend upward and my heart to sing songs I'd forgotten I knew.

Praise and faith work hand in hand. God multiplies my faith when I praise Him. The more I praise, the greater I trust Him to help me. And as a result, the more I have cause to praise Him. And with that trust comes patience. When I know God is leading, I cease to try to rush Him or sway Him to my own thinking.

Praise helps me hear His voice more clearly. With my selfish thoughts out of the way, I can discover what it is He wants me to know. In praise I often find the answers to my most weighty questions. But remember, God doesn't tell you what He's going to do for you; He tells you who He is. And this makes all the difference.

A Christian philosopher once said, "When I need faith, there are two steps to take: go to God's Word and begin praising Him. The two go together as naturally as hydrogen and oxygen make water."

Oswald Chambers, author of *My Utmost for His Highest,* wrote: "A saint's life is in the hands of God like a bow and arrow in the hands of an archer. God is aiming at something the saint cannot see, and He stretches and strains, and every now and again, the saint says—'I cannot stand any more.' Faith is not a pathetic sentiment, but robust vigorous confidence built on the fact that God is holy love. . . . Faith is the heroic effort of your life, you fling yourself in reckless confidence on God. . . . If we take this view, life becomes one great romance, a glorious opportunity for seeing marvelous things all the time" (Oswald Chambers, *My Utmost for His Highest* [Ulrichsville, Ohio: Barbour and Co., 1963], p. 93).

Praise is total confidence in God, a no-holds-barred declaration that God has everything under control. I don't need to be the Little Engine That Could and repeat again and again, "I think

I can, I think I can," until I succeed. Because as any saint knows, I can't do anything—at least, not alone.

In her book *The Summer of the Great-Grandmother* Madeleine L'Engle wrote: "I learn slowly and always the hard way. Trying to be something I am not and cannot be, is not only arrogant, it is stupid" (p. 49).

So don't talk to me about self-confidence. My self-confidence will send me flat on my face. But with God-confidence "I can do all things." Guaranteed!

You see the phrase "No fear" everywhere—on T-shirts, on baseball caps, on car windshields and the bumpers of vans. Wouldn't it be great if it were true? To live in a world of no fear? But ours is a world gone mad, a world in which preschoolers get gunned down while riding the teeter-totter, teens' greatest worry is they won't see their twentieth birthday, or a shopper will go way out of his or her way to avoid walking near a gang of kids standing on a street corner.

Each morning we awaken to an unpredictable day filled with surprises, trials, and anxieties. You might get hit by a car, fired from your job, mugged on the street, robbed in your home, slandered by a friend, sued by a neighbor, or have your stocks plummet in value.

So why did you get up this morning? Many people ask themselves that every day. They live in a constant state of fear. And fear brings trauma, inner stress. Mental stress leads to sickness and death. As you paw through the dumpsters of your mind, you know that you are creating unnecessary stress for yourself, but the negative adrenaline produced by the activity gives you a false charge. Thomas Carlyle advised us to get rid of fear. "Yeah, right!" you say.

The psalmist declared in Psalm 56:3: "What time I am afraid, I will trust in Thee" (KJV). The author of Hebrews wrote: "Never will I leave you; never will I forsake you" (Heb. 13:5). If you believe God's Word, then you must claim His promises for the very real fears in your life. God isn't a part-time deity, nor is He out to get me. And He can't be bribed. His Word can be trusted.

The devil seeks to remove the Word of God from us, especially the good news of salvation. As he did Jesus in the wilderness, he attacks our faith by casting aspersions on God. Satan tries to disarm us of the sword of the Spirit because he knows that my God is "able to do immeasurably more than all we ask or imagine" (Eph. 3:20). He recognizes that if he can get us to doubt God's promises, we are susceptible to his temptations.

I love popcorn. But for me to take out a package of microwavable popcorn and put it in the microwave takes a bit of faith. I must believe in Orville Redenbacher (or at least in his reputation), the grocer, and my microwave or I wouldn't make a move toward satisfying my urge for popcorn. Imagine the faith it takes to look at one of those tiny yellow kernels and expect that by adding heat I will get a satisfying bite of popped corn. I don't ever remember sticking the popcorn bag in the microwave and closing the door, setting the timer, then agonizing over whether or not I would get to enjoy the desired treat. I simply trusted that I would. And if I'm going to share that popped corn with someone, I might even say, "This is the greatest popcorn on the market today. Wait till you see the size of the popped corn." When I do so I am not only praising the corn itself, but also praising the popcorn grower, the genetic developer, and good old Mr. Redenbacher for selling such a fine product.

By speaking words of praise and by claiming biblical scripture, I am not merely reaffirming sweet, positive ideas that may or may not correspond to reality. What I am doing is declaring to the unfallen universe, to Satan and his host of demons, and to my own old sinful nature, "Taste and see that the Lord is good. I will glorify His holy name. He's my Father, and I can trust Him."

Three

More Than a Chorus Line

"Hallelujah! It's a good thing to sing praise to our God; praise is beautiful, praise is fitting."
—Psalm 147:1, Message

When I was 9 or 10 my best friend, Patty, her sister Helen, and I got a "kick" out of watching the Rockettes dance troupe on television. Of course, we had to try to imitate them. The three of us would form a chorus line on my parents' front lawn. Kick, one, two, kick, three, four, kick. Dozens of kicks and bruises later we'd end up rolling on the ground and laughing until our sides ached. We couldn't get synchronized, no matter how hard we tried.

For some people, praise is a chorus line, a delightful little ditty you sing between services at church each week because others are doing it. To others, praise is the ditty itself. And for yet others, praise is a byword, a phrase of explanation or something we insert into our conversation to replace a less desirable epithet.

You know what I mean. You're driving in heavy traffic and a driver cuts in front of you. Slamming on your brakes, you miss hitting the other car with mere inches to spare. With a gasp you say, "Praise God. I almost hit that guy! What a jerk." Little more than a habit.

Genuine praise must be more than all of these. The biblical concept of praise has become to me one of the most important principles of the kingdom of God. For when people praise God, miracles happen. To praise God is to salute Him, to acknowledge His majesty and power.

A preacher friend described a dream he once had. In it he visited heaven. His guardian angel took him on a tour through the Holy City to the magnificent river of life. Seeing the river's incredible beauty, he breathed, "Praise God." Instantly all the creatures of heaven stopped what they were doing. The lions awoke from their naps. The lambs paused from their cavorting on the cool green grass. People from other planets halted their sightseeing. And the angels laid down their harps. All creation lifted its voice in joyous praise to the King of kings, the Lord of lords. The rafters of heaven rang with their praise. The minister's point was that "heaven takes praise seriously."

So what constitutes praise to God? The Bible says that our praise can be as loud as a clanging cymbal or a sounding trumpet (Ps. 150:1-6). Or it can be as quiet as a baby's breath. God loves both. He always honors sincere praise.

Praise is an act of respect to the Father. When we show honor and respect, we will receive honor and respect (1 Sam. 2:30). At times God adds to our praise. He rejoices over us with singing (Zeph. 3:17). I like that. I wonder what part God sings in? Bass, tenor, alto, soprano? Maybe all four.

Psalm 148 reminds us that all creation praises God: the fish, the birds, the monkeys, even the inanimate aspects of His creation, such as the sun and the moon. On my radio show I love to play a children's song called "Who's the King of the Jungle?" In a simple way it's a song designed to praise our heavenly Father.

Isn't it strange that of all God's creatures, from manatees to squid, from microscopic protozoa to the gargantuan whale, it is the one designed in God's image who alone has trouble remembering how great God really is?

My dad was a contractor. Often he helped refurbish old houses. One day he salvaged several grime-covered crystal icicles from an old chandelier about to be destroyed. He gave them to me. After cleaning them in hot sudsy water, I held one of them up to the sunlight. To my delight, the different facets of the cut glass created a brilliant rainbow of light on my mother's floor.

The more I've studied into praise and rejoicing, the more facets of God's gift I've come to appreciate. Here are just a few.

Praise is a spiritual offering to God (Heb. 13:15).

Praise acknowledges the abundance of gifts that God gives to us (Ps. 103:2).

Praise and forgiveness are inseparable (Ps. 65:1-3). One of the definitions of the Greek word for praise is "confess." We are never closer to God than when we confess our sins to Him and admit that He alone is faithful, pure, and holy.

Praise recognizes God's power as Creator (Isa. 40:27-31, TLB).

Praise is a choice that we make, not a passive response to a good deed or a compliment (Ps. 34:1-3).

Praise is a daily activity for the child of God (Ps. 61:8). I'm not a morning person. Before 10:00 a.m. I'm useless. When I get calls too early in the morning, I'll forget everything that is said. But since I asked the Holy Spirit to make praise be my first thought in the morning and my last thought at night, I find pleasure upon waking, whether it be 6:00 a.m. or 9:00.

Praise turns grief into joy (Ps. 30:11, 12).

God "inhabitest the praises" of His people (Ps. 22:3, KJV).

Praise takes you into the very presence of God (Ps. 100:4).

Praise identifies you as God's child (1 Peter 2:9).

Praise can do all that and more! Here are just a few testimonies to the miracle of praise:

William Law, an English cleric of the eighteenth century, said, "If anyone could tell you the shortest, surest way to all happiness and perfection, he must tell you to make it a rule to yourself to thank and praise God for everything that happens to you. For whatever calamity that happens to you, if you thank and praise God for it, you turn it into a blessing."

Helen Keller wrote, "I thank God for my handicaps, for through them I have found myself, my work, and my God."

Ellen White commented that "the worship of God consists chiefly of praise and prayer. Every follower of Christ should engage in this worship. No one can sing by proxy, bear testimony by proxy, or pray by proxy. As a rule, too many dark testimonies are borne in social service, savoring more of murmuring than of gratitude and praise" (*Review and Herald,* Jan. 1, 1880).

When I think of the great Reformer Martin Luther, I imagine a staid and dour individual, a man capable of heaving his inkwell at a wall because he believed he saw the devil standing there laughing at him. Luther's wife had to remind him to smile. So the last thing I expected to find was that the first hymn he wrote was one of praise, entitled "Dear Christian One and All Rejoice."

After reading *On Wings of Praise,* an acquaintance of mine commented, "All this talk of happy religion comes from fuzzy-headed theologians!"

I smiled to myself. I wanted to say, but didn't, "Yes, that's right, fuzzy-headed theologians like the apostle Paul who wrote, 'Rejoice in the Lord alway: and again I say, Rejoice!' [Phil. 4:4, KJV]. If that's fuzzy-headed theology, I'll take it. I always wanted curly hair anyway!"

Recently some close friends of ours went through the devastation of job loss. Their situation was similar to what Richard and I had also experienced a few years back. Through the months of stress we tried to be there for Jason and Lila. We listened, we cried, we prayed with them. (Isn't it beautiful how God equips us beforehand with the understanding necessary to come to the aid of our brothers and sisters when they're in pain?)

We shared our experience of how God led us through our own difficulty. Jason stayed with us until we began talking about the concept of praise—the biggest, most exciting change that had occurred in our lives.

"I can't buy it," he protested. "How can one praise God for

bad things that happen in life? Isn't that an effort to manipulate Him, just as spoiled children try to manipulate their parents to get their own way? Isn't your praising just another game?"

His words startled me as I recalled all the games I had played to win God's favor: Mary Martyr, Pastor Pull-Apart, Pin the Tail on the Heretic, Busy Bee Me—my list was endless. I also remembered the discouragement I felt when each game failed to bring me the comfort I needed. Had I, I asked myself, exchanged old games for a new one—one that, when all was said and done, would leave me equally as empty and hopeless as before? Was I playing the conniving little girl trying to sweet-talk her Father into an advance on next month's allowance? Were all my praises a gimmick to get all I could out of the "Old Man"?

I turned to my Bible for answers. After all, that was where I had first discovered the importance of praise in a Christian's life. In it the words of David, Paul, Isaiah, and Zephaniah had turned my life around. The paradigm shift had not only changed my life but had saved it. I'm not talking about a 20-minute songfest at the beginning of church each week, but of incorporating praise into every facet of my life. First Peter 2:9 identifies God's people and their reason for existence as "that you may declare the praises of him who called you out of darkness into his wonderful light." God had certainly done that—taken me from abject darkness to iridescent light. As a result I discovered a new purpose to my being—to bring glory and honor to His name in all things.

I reread the words of Romans 12:2: "Do not conform any longer to the pattern of this world, but be transformed by the renewing of your mind." I decided again to go over the 359 praise verses I'd first read on the subject. This time I added all the texts containing the words "hallelujah," "hosanna," "glory," and "rejoice" as well. I read in the Old Testament how God accused His people of committing such sins as idolatry, immorality, homosexuality, and sodomy. One of the items on His list was ingrati-

tude. They had failed to remember the benefits God had bestowed on them.

The psalms of David depicted a man who knew how to
praise! I said aloud the praises of Isaiah. I reread the story of
Mary and her prayer of rejoicing. I sang hosannas with the angels
at Jesus' birth. My heart soared with the praise directed to the
Philippians: "Rejoice in the Lord always" (Phil. 4:4). Not sometimes! Not only on good-hair days. But always!

My search took me through the testaments to the book of
Revelation. Even there the command to praise is evident. "Fear
God and give him glory, because the hour of his judgment has
come. Worship him who made the heavens, the earth, the sea
and the springs of water" (Rev. 14:7).

So often I'd read that text and concentrated on the "hour of
judgment." I would get caught up in the coming judgment and
miss what He said to do about it—give God glory, praise Him.

Give God glory—that's praise. Worship Him—that's
praise. Eventually I realized that I couldn't do anything about
the coming judgment and that God wasn't asking me to. What
He was requesting of me was to praise Him. Praise is the message He wants me to understand as I tiptoe around the rim of
the third millennium.

Throughout history God has had a people that praised
Him. Now, at such a crucial time in earth's history, the church
is rediscovering praise as the Christian's ID and inheritance.
Praise opens heaven's gates, not bringing heaven down to the
church, but lifting the chuch out of the miasma of this earth
toward heaven.

Praise is a new way of thinking, acting, and talking that drives
away the old fears. The praising child takes God's tens of thousands
of promises seriously. He or she believes every word that comes
from God's mouth. If God says that He "inhabiteth the praises" of
His people (Ps. 22:3, KJV) then He does put His presence in the
praise of His children. If God says it's true, then it is. Simple as that.

And if God lifts you up on the wings of praise to His kingdom, imagine living continually surrounded by His creative energy. As I live in His kingdom, then He lives in me, and we complete a circle of praise.

When Jesus walked the rocky paths of Galilee, He praised His Father. Everything He said or did glorified God. That was His purpose for being here—to glorify His Father. Praise was foremost in His mind. When I praise, I invite Christ's mind to be in me. And all of heaven rejoices. Even when I idly say, "Praise God!" I disrupt heaven's calm. Heavenly beings take their praises seriously.

Some people become nervous when Christians talk about Christ living in them. They mistake the scriptural truth for the New Age philosophy of "God lives in me, hence I am God." Quite the contrary. Praise puts me in proper perspective with God's holiness and my sinfulness. When I address Him with praise, I confess my true condition. I know I am not God when I see His goodness and His faithfulness in my life.

Every day it seems I break promises, some I made to myself and some to others. I tell shady truths and weasel out of tasks I prefer not to do. Yet my God is always faithful. He never abandons me. There's "no shadow of turning," as the old hymn goes. He always comes through for me. All the pride and false assumptions I have about myself become visible in the light of my Father's goodness when I bow and gratefully praise Him. It's on my knees that I can best appreciate His goodness. And it's from my knees that He lifts me out of my circumstances and into His presence.

Long before I finished my search for answers, I knew that praising was not just another game for me. It was what God wanted me to do. I can't speak for Jason, but I certainly can for myself. Instead of being the whinings of a spoiled daughter as my friend implied, my praise gives the faith dwelling in my heart a voice. Praise is the spoken word for the God-seeded trust that He planted in me.

Sitting on my kitchen windowsill are two avocado pits that I intend to start growing one of these days. This morning one pit cracked open. The tiny cell of life inside that hard shell was too eager to wait for me. Faith is like that. It can't be kept inside or it will wither and die. I must express it. Praise is its vehicle of expression.

Whether in adversity or prosperity, my praise announces to the universe that my heavenly Father is the greatest, that He loves me and keeps His word. My praise pokes a finger in Satan's eye and puts him in his place. Thanks to Christ, the cross, and His resurrection, I can have victory over Satan and his dastardly demons at every turn. Praise God!

Upside Down, Right Side Up

"Though the fig tree does not bud and there are no grapes on the vines, though the olive crop fails and the fields produce no food, though there are no sheep in the pen and no cattle in the stalls, yet I will rejoice in the Lord, I will be joyful in God my Savior."
—Habakkuk 3:17, 18

D oesn't make sense, does it, being joyful in God when life is falling down around your ears, as my grandma used to say? Living in California's great Central Valley, where the local economy depends on the olive trees bearing olives and grapes producing raisins and wine, I can understand Habakkuk's words of praise. Several years ago a freeze eliminated the orange crop, and the industry is still recouping its loss. So when the prophet says, "Yet I will . . . be joyful in God, my Savior," I can relate.

We know little about Habakkuk except that he was a contemporary of Jeremiah. Habakkuk's vigorous faith was rooted in his God. The wickedness in Israel perplexed the prophet. But in his book Habakkuk learns to rest in God's perfect timing in a spirit of worship. His attitude in the last few verses is upside down compared to the world's logic. His praise appears to be that of a fool.

I love the idea of camping—roughing it out in God's natural world, inhaling fresh aromas, seeing glorious vistas of God's creative power as I commune with beast and bush. It's the reality of camping that bothers me, especially at 3:00 a.m., when I inevitably awaken and realize that I must climb out of my comfy sleeping bag, put on my slippers and robe, and stumble 100 feet or so to the nearest cement block building marked "Ladies."

The Rizzo-Krueger family had chosen Capitol Reef National Park as the rendezvous point for the in-laws and outlaws to meet—rather appropriate, don't you think, since the sequestered little valley in the center of the park was where the notorious Butch Cassidy and his gang hid out from the law.

Sleep came easy after a day of hiking on the rocks and an evening of s'mores and Uno around the campfire. Then around 3:00 a.m. the inevitable happened. For a while I tried to convince myself that I didn't have to get up, that I could wait until morning. I failed. Grudgingly I crawled out of my warm sleeping bag, put on my robe and slippers, and made the trek across the campground to the little gray building.

Once inside, I'd barely closed the stall door behind me when someone entered the stall next to me. I glanced down at the floor and immediately recognized a pair of parrot-green sneakers with orange swooshes.

Before we left on our vacation, my 12-year-old daughter, Rhonda, had gone shopping for new sneakers, sans mother. Her eyes danced with excitement when she arrived home and showed me her purchase—parrot-green sneakers with orange swooshes. I choked. Never before had I seen parrot-green and orange sneakers in the shape of experimental trapezoids.

Knowing she was eager for my approval, I had to think quickly. Grateful the shoes were for everyday wear and not for church, I said, "Wow, they're certainly colorful. Which of your outfits do you plan to wear them with?" In my mind I reviewed her wardrobe of feminine blues and pinks.

Her smile broadened. "Aren't they pretty? They'll go with everything!" I would soon learn how right she was. She did wear them with everything!

And here the green trapezoidal sneakers were in the next stall, orange swooshes and all. Now, I admit, I have a penchant for teasing. I love to tease those I love. (I do try to curb my teasing when I'm around strangers, although I don't always succeed.) I tease my kids, my husband, and our cat, Max. In response to my teasing, Max scratches, Richard growls, and my kids beg for mercy. Corky, our deceased Sheltie, loved to be as close to me as possible until I began teasing, then he would drag himself to his feet and move to the other side of the room.

Regardless of the hour, I had to tease my daughter. After all, I might know her identity, but she had no idea who I was. After thinking for a moment about what I could do, my gaze rested on the roll of toilet paper.

Tearing sheets of toilet paper into pieces, I rolled the paper into pebble-sized balls. Placing one of them on the palm of my left hand, I took the thumb and index finger of my right hand and flicked the paper over the top of the dividing wall. Nothing happened. No sound came from the stall beside me. I repeated my action a second and a third time—again no response. Disgusted, I tossed the entire handful of toilet paper pebbles over the wall. Still nothing! Not a sound.

"Oh, Rhonda," I mumbled. "I'm not going to stay here all night!" Extending my left foot beneath the divider, I stomped on the closest parrot-green sneaker. Instantly the shoe's owner snatched her foot to the other side of her stall. That's when my first doubt hit me. As the idea tumbled around my sleepy brain, I argued, *No! It couldn't be.* It had never occurred to me that I could be wrong. *Surely there can't be two people in this tiny campground wearing trapezoidal parrot-green sneakers with orange swooshes on the sides!*

How embarrassing, I thought. I started to giggle, then snort, then laugh aloud. The person in the stall beside me shot from the stall like a greyhound at the starting block. Knowing I had to apologize and explain my bizarre behavior, I hurried out of my stall. I caught her at the sink. At the sight of me standing between herself and the only exit, she gaped at me in horror, like a deer caught in car headlights.

"I'm so sorry," I began. Unfortunately, I have a problem with laughter. Once I start I can't stop. So my apology must have sounded something like: "I thought you were my d-d-au-au-au-te-hee-hee-hee . . ." I doubled over with laughter. When I paused to gasp for air, the woman charged past me and disappeared into the night. It set off a new round of hilarity.

I tried to compose myself before leaving the restroom, but, as I said earlier, once I start laughing I can't always stop. This was definitely one of those times. All the way back to our campsite I giggled. And you know how noise travels in the night? Flashlights blinked on across the campgrounds. Campers grumbled and grunted, but nothing could silence me.

As I passed my daughters' sleeping bags, I heard Rhonda say to her sister, Kelli, "Oh, no, Mama's at it again."

Much to my husband's chagrin, it took more than 30 minutes for my laughter to subside and allow him to go back to sleep.

Strange how I was so sure it was Rhonda in the next stall. Unfortunately, I was wrong. But the story doesn't end here. Ironically, the first person I met the next morning as I headed into the restroom was the sneaker woman. Taking one look at me, she shot out of the building. I've never seen a 70-year-old woman run so fast in my life.

Mistakes? Of course, we all make them. They are a part of being human. Studies say that one out of every six choices a person makes will probably be wrong. My husband vows that my averages are more like one in four or one in three, and he's probably right, considering that I've been known to climb into a stranger's car by mistake, pick up the wrong handbag by accident, or run the full length of a college campus with my skirt tucked into my panty hose.

Pretty lousy averages, even for the most careful among us.

You buy the brown pumps and realize the black ones would have gone with more outfits. Or you run a yellow light with a police car directly behind you. For more than an hour you wait for a friend, only to learn later that you were at the wrong mall.

Alas, we must live with our mistakes. Some are easier to cope with than others. The brown pumps collect dust in the back of your closet. An apology corrects the mall misunderstanding, and the traffic violation ups your car insurance. And you learn from your experience, right? Hopefully.

In the case of the parrot-green sneaker incident, not only have I discovered the dangers of leaping to conclusions, but also I've made several hundred dollars off that story. Its first publication was in an April Fool's Day issue of *Redbook,* entitled "My Most Embarrassing Moments." I only hope the victim of my misdirected joke read the story and got a good laugh from it as well.

Yes, I was so certain I was right. Both instinct and logic told me I was right. After all, what are the chances of two females wearing the same trapezoidal parrot-green sneakers with orange swooshes while camping in such a remote area of southern Utah? I am certain the calculation would have corroborated my conclusion that such a coincidence would be negligible at the most. But I was wrong—dead wrong. All the logic in the world, all the personal opinions I might have, all the common sense I could claim, didn't turn the victim of my misguided humor into my daughter.

While growing older and hopefully wiser, I've discovered more often than not that my common sense, my logic, and my personal opinions are too often upside down and inside out to reality—God's reality. What God sees in me as obstinate weakness, I call a strength.

The results can be worse in the interpersonal realm. When I trust my wits instead of God's, I must live with the sinful consequences.

All the guiding principles of His Word are oxymorons when viewed from human reason. The last shall be first. Any 10-year-old will tell you that if you wait to be last, they'll run out of Klondike bars. The poor shall inherit the earth? Tell that one to Bill Gates or Donald Trump. Lose your life for God's sake and you will find it. Are you kidding? You'd better look out for number one or no one else will. Sow in tears, you'll reap joy? Nonsense. Forget the tears. You gotta make your own happiness in life.

Faith can move mountains? To move a mountain takes direction, planning, dedication, determination, and brute force. Turn the other cheek? Mess with me and I'll give you cheek! Cast your bread upon the waters and it will return to you? Yeah, all you'll get back is soggy bread.

If you gain the whole world, how can you lose your soul? Ever try shoving a camel through the eye of a needle? Become as a little child? Are you kidding?

Competition and getting ahead were as much a part of Jesus' world as they are of ours. Like us, individuals in His day were constantly thinking of ways of surpassing others, of dominating, controlling, and making more money. Leave the mundane tasks to lesser persons, such as women, eunuchs, and children.

The people seated on the grassy slope listened to Jesus' words but couldn't understand. The disciples shuddered at what the wise men of their community must be thinking when Jesus took a little child onto His lap. *Hold a child in Your lap?* the disciples thought. Caring for children was women's work. Women chattered about babies while men discussed the weightier matters of life. It was a woman's task to simplify her husband's or father's life so he could be religious.

Jesus continued by saying, "Whoever receives one of these little children in My name receives Me" (Mark 9:37, NKJV). It made no sense to their "men's club" mentality. Of all God's creatures, human infants are the most helpless for the longest length of time. Colts walk within minutes of their birth, while insects and fish need no adult supervision. In first-century Jewish society power was only an adult male's prerogative. Jesus' followers expected Him to speak of mighty warriors and battle regalia. They longed for a charismatic political leader who could liberate the Jewish people. All this talk of an inner kingdom and babies baffled them.

"You must become as a little child to enter the kingdom of God? Is that what He just said? Doesn't He realize that children are at the bottom of our society's social status, right down there with women, publicans, and lepers?"

Imagine if Jesus had said, "To enter God's kingdom, you must become a leper." Or "To enter My kingdom, you must become a woman." Either statement would have been revolutionary, if not impossible for the disciples to comprehend.

Of what value is a child? Children are a drain on the finances, at least until old enough to do their share of the work! "The judicial obligation to maintain children came to an end when they reached the age of six; boys could be sent away from home to learn a trade and girls could be sold as slaves" (Joseph F. Grassi, *Mary Magdalene and the Women in Jesus' Life* [Cambridge University Press: 1984], p. 53).

Jesus was speaking to the hearts of women that day as well. The world of women and children was one in which inconspicuous little services mattered and reached to the very heart of the kingdom. Most men found it difficult to understand the concepts of doing for others or of service without recognition, because they were simply not involved in such things on a regular basis—if at all (*ibid.*, p. 136). Jesus knew that His disciples were so stuck in the male competitive world that they would need to be shocked into seeing things as heaven sees them. His disciples couldn't believe that they would actually have to be with children and watch them to learn what God's kingdom was all about.

For Jesus the child is one who doesn't know the meaning of the word impossible, one who lives in a world of wonder, a world not yet encrusted by the adult tendency to turn everything into the ordinary and routine. Jesus laughed and played with children, for this is what God's kingdom was all about—spontaneity. Living in the moment is what Jesus wanted His disciples to learn. The kingdom of God is right here—a lesson we still have trouble understanding (*ibid.*, p. 76).

To Jesus the most important matter was liberate not only women but men! Men needed to enter the inner world of love and service much more than women did the outer world of men, which was so often a dead-end street (*ibid.*, p. 75).

Jesus' great miracle of feeding the 5,000 began with a child. The practical disciples advised Him to send the people home. "It's getting late. Besides, where could we get enough food for so many people? It would take 200 days' wages' worth of bread to feed them all." The next street corner had no McDonald's or Taco Bell.

But in His audience one young child understood what Jesus was saying. In faith the boy brought his five barley loaves and two fishes to the Master. They weren't uniformly sliced supermarket loaves, but the small flat pancake-type loaves he stored in his leather pouch on his belt as a kind of picnic lunch.

The crowd must have tittered with laughter when they learned of his offer. How absurd for the child to do such a thing. The boy might have blushed with discomfort and tried to slip away. But the joke was on the grown-ups.

The child didn't know the meaning of the word impossible. He was willing to share his food in obedience to Jesus' word: "Give them to eat" (*ibid.*, p.77).

Often I hear the topic of giving to the "undesirables" discussed among the "brethren." "How do I know when to give and when my money will be wasted?" someone always asks. I feel uncomfortable with that question. Jesus said, "Give ye them to eat," no strings attached. My job is done. Responsibility for that gift is no longer mine once I carry out God's commission.

With a grateful smile Jesus accepted the loaves from the boy and began giving them to everyone until all had eaten their fill.

"The child had taught them how to do away with world hunger; by trusting that there is enough food for everyone if we only begin to share and then let this contagious miracle of sharing spread through all the world" (*ibid.*, p.77).

Not only did Jesus do the impossible with one boy's lunch, but He did the unthinkable as well. He told the disciples to distribute the bread. Serve food? That's women's work! Christ's weary and somewhat miffed friends must have stared in horror at His suggestion. Weren't there enough women here to perform such a chore? Now He's asking us to serve women and children? What's next? Bus the tables later? Pass the Rolaids.

The Jews of Jesus' day did not permit women and children to eat with men in public (see notes on Matthew 14:21 in the NIV study Bible). The men believed themselves destined to become secretaries in the Messiah's royal cabinet, generals of His victorious army. They must have wondered, *Doesn't He see the very real world around us? Is He so spiritual, so otherworldly, that He's blind to reality and customs?*

Jesus saw and understood the inequities of the sinful world all too well. He knew that unless His disciples learned to see the reality of God's kingdom, they would miss out on eternity.

As He walked through the narrow streets of His country, His heart ached for the hurting and the hungry. The extremes of riches and poverty accosted Him on every street corner. As He strolled past rows of dilapidated houses, He saw the ill-clad children playing in the gutters. His pace must have been slowed by beggars, some blind, some disabled, and felt His heart touched.

Jesus lived in a land of injustice. Anyone He might ask, whether it be a child on the street, a woman at the town well, or a merchant in his stand, would have blamed Rome. But the Son of God understood that their prison was one of the mind, not the body. The shackles holding people down were greed and hate, not a Roman despot. He knew the truth, and He knew truth would set them free.

But to discover such freeing truth, they would need to acquire the heart and the spirit of a child—not one old enough to doubt or to have become cynical.

"He called a little child and had him stand among them. And he said: 'I tell you the truth, unless you change and become like little children, you will never enter the kingdom of heaven. Therefore, whoever humbles himself like this child is the greatest in the kingdom of heaven'" (Matt. 18:2-4).

In place of the term *children*, some translations use *infants*. Tiny babies? No wonder the disciples and the people assembled on that grassy hillside found His words hard to swallow. Who would want to become a mewling and drooling, bald and toothless, spit-uppy, diaper-wearing, helpless baby?

As much as I love babies, I wouldn't want to return to that state. I treasure my independence, my hand-eye coordination, my sense of balance, my abilities that allow me self-control. Exactly. The skill I treasure most can also be the thing that keeps me from the kingdom. Jesus understood the nature of a child. Until life ingrains suspicion and distrust, a child will naturally trust. Children have no guile. Their innocent faith and honesty is what the Saviour wants to restore in us.

As I mentioned at the beginning of this book, a baby recently joined our household. My daughter Kelli gave birth to our first grandchild, Jarod Michael. In her ministry's newsletter she wrote, "God is already using Jarod to teach us more about Him. I heard it said that when I look into the pure, innocent eyes of my baby, I see the same look of innocence God sees when He looks at me every morning, for His mercies are 'new every morning'! Wow! Thank You for Your grace, God!" Each of us can possess the innocence of an infant every day. I like that.

Art Linkletter built a career on the innocent and often humorous remarks of children. Bill Cosby continued the tradition on his TV specials. Never ask a child a question to which you desire something other than the truth.

When my daughter Rhonda was a preschooler, she came

upon a woman in a public restroom applying heavy blue eyeshadow to her eyelids. Rhonda had never seen anything like this before. "Why are you painting your eyelids?" the child asked.

The woman smiled down at her and replied, "It's to make my eyes pretty."

With the naïveté of childhood, Rhonda said, "Well, it doesn't!"

During Christ's triumphal entry into Jerusalem, the children baffled the Pharisees. They shouted, "Hosanna to the Son of David" (Matt. 21:15). The religious leaders were indignant. They reprimanded Jesus for the children's noise. "Do you hear what these children are saying?" they demanded (verse 16). (*Hosanna* is Aramaic for "Save us." They were asking Jesus to save them, recognizing His power and love.)

"Yes," He replied. "Have you never read, 'From the lips of children and infants you have ordained praise'?" (verse 16).

Praise bubbles out of a child's heart. Listen to 5-year-olds as they study the face of a daisy or consider the mysteries of a wooly bear caterpillar. God ordains the praise of little children. And it is only as we are reborn into His kingdom that we can recapture the pure joy bound in a child's heart.

The Kingdom of Praise

"But seek first his kingdom and his righteousness, and all these things will be given to you as well."
—Matthew 6:33

Kids and adults alike love to visit the Magical Kingdom of Disneyland. The Disney organization has turned the idea of the happiest place on earth into a multimillion-dollar concern. And why not? That's what corporations are in the business to do—to make money. Recently I visited Epcot Center, a Disney derivative in Orlando, Florida. I couldn't believe the amount of merchandise available to the visitor. Every shop—and there were dozens—held a wild array of brightly colored objects for sale.

God has a kingdom, not of magic, sleight-of-hand, or plastic facades. It's not a world of fast-food stands or umbrella-covered ice-cream carts. Nor is it a place where whistles toot and carousels whirl in wild abandon.

Some people would have you believe it is just a place to look forward to, a utopia where we'll sit on clouds and sip virgin piña coladas. Others see their nirvana filled with lollypop trees and candy-cane mountains. Yet the kingdom of God is so much more than a never-never land of childish dreams and unreasonable wishes.

The reality is that God's kingdom is here and now. While

Disney's kingdom closes at midnight and all the fairy-tale characters change into blue jeans and T-shirts and drive home, I can live in God's kingdom 24 hours a day, seven days a week—through the wonder of praise.

When I began praising, I discovered that incredible joy was available to me even in my messiest here and now. My life could be crumbling around me. Satan's destruction could be closing in on me, yet I could be at total peace, safe and secure in God's holy kingdom of grace.

As I choose to praise, a new way of thinking emerges, a paradigm shift occurs in my brain, and I experience the Father's kingdom regardless of my circumstance.

The word "kingdom" is a slightly misleading translation of the Greek word *Basileia* or the Hebrew term *Malkut*. The kingdom isn't a static or territorial state, but a dynamic symbol of God actively reigning now, "the sphere of God's rule, where His rule is acknowledged and His people submit to His rule" (Morris Maddox, *The Christian Healing Ministry* [London: SPCK, 1981], p. 27). Imagine the creative power found in such a place.

The Bible speaks of two kingdoms of God. It's interesting to note that the kingdom of heaven is always the kingdom of God, but the kingdom of God is not limited to the kingdom of heaven until they become one at the marriage of the Lamb of God.

The noun used for the future kingdom is a "point tense," or a sudden event as found in Matthew 6:10. However, the noun for the kingdom mentioned in Romans 14:17 is present tense, meaning that it exists today. A place of peace, joy, and righteousness here and now, it is the kingdom Jesus sent His disciples forth to preach, the kingdom declared after the resurrection (Acts 1:3). It is the kingdom the poor inherit, the kingdom where I can choose to live.

"Except ye be converted, and become as little children . . ." (Matt. 28:3, KJV). Only a "born again" child of God can understand this kingdom (John 3:10-12). When we're born again, or as some prefer to call it, "born from above," we're not "adopted" into God's family, but are blood-born through the sacrificial blood of Jesus Christ. We're family in the highest sense.

Larry Crane, a pastor friend of mine, tells how when Andrea, their oldest daughter, was adopted, the hospital recorded her adoption and the names of her biological parents, but the Crane family records list Andrea as naturally born into their family, with all the privileges and responsibilities such an honor entails—a Crane through and through.

You and I were born again into God's family, not biologically, but we are just as secure because of His birth and His sacrifice. For that reason I can enjoy family life in abundance (John 10:10). That abundance is available for all family members but is most enjoyed by those who choose to set up residence in God's kingdom.

What if the Cranes had adopted Andrea, made her completely theirs, but as a child she chose to live elsewhere? She would still be a Crane, but because of her living arrangements she wouldn't get to enjoy the day-by-day benefits of being a Crane. She might hear about the great times the Crane family have. And she might even get to visit the family once or twice a week, but part-time habitation doesn't compensate for the absence of full-time abundant life in the Crane household. There's no comparison.

Oswald Chambers, in his book *My Utmost for His Highest,* says on page 267 that "if we are born again it is the easiest thing to live in a right relationship to God and the most difficult thing to go wrong."

In our materialistic world we, as children of God, have no words to describe His creative presence in our lives. Very real changes occur in the heart and mind of those who choose to live in the center of their Father's love.

As in Jesus' day, a very real world of fear surrounds the child of God. Fear of failure, fear of the future, fear of abandonment, fear of death, fear of poverty, fear of growing old, and the list goes on. We humans scamper about in our own little worlds, clawing and grubbing from one day to the next, collecting baubles and trophies to affirm our greatness and to suppress the fears that haunt us day and night.

Some years ago the statement "No fear!" became popular. You still see the words emblazoned on everything from trucks to T-shirts. How ironic. Never has a generation been more imprisoned by their own fears. Violence on the street and in the school yard threatens our very existence.

We of the older generations wag our heads in disgust at the spiked hair, nose earrings, and ghoulish makeup some choose to exhibit. Yet we conveniently forget that it was our generations who supplied the drugs, created the horror flicks, and produced the porno magazines. It was we who created the world of divorce, downsizing, and rampant indebtedness. No fear?

And all the bravado inherent in their "No fear" logos doesn't quiet the fear gnawing at their insides and crippling their creativity. They've never learned that "perfect love casts out fear" (1 John 4:18, NKJV), because they've not seen such love in the world around them.

Earlier generations struggled with the same problem. I know—I've been there. I remember when my future seemed so bleak that I saw little reason to go on living. The father of lies had twisted my thinking into believing that my family would be better off without me. I was afraid to live, yet afraid that if I tried to end it all, I'd botch the job and end up in a worse state.

Ah, you think, *that could never happen to me. I'm too strong, being made of sterner stuff.* That's what I once thought too. After all, I come from pioneer stock. I can trace my roots back to before the Revolutionary War—fighters all! Yet when my time of trouble dawned, I yearned to fold up my tent and creep away to a desolate canyon somewhere where no one could find me.

As I've traveled around the country speaking to women's

groups, I've discovered that, at one time or another, most women have considered committing suicide. Often someone attending the conference has entertained such ideas within the previous week. And interestingly, their thoughts have echoed mine. Imagine Satan convincing us that our last act of kindness should be self-destruction. Talk about twisting love inside out!

Intellectually I was a daughter of the King of the universe. As a child I sang "Jesus Loves Me" as loudly as did the other children. Hadn't I testified to others of God's glory and peace? Yet in the throes of discouragement, fear replaced joy, discouragement shoved aside hope, and a death wish overtook my natural exuberance for living and loving.

That I mentioned much of this in my earlier book *On Wings of Praise* is no accident. I don't apologize. I believe such a discovery is important enough for a second look.

The advice in Revelation 3:11 to let no one "take your crown" (NKJV) played around in my mind. Although enemies tried to destroy my family and my life, I would not let them take my crown as well. God took this little flicker of faith and warmed my wounded soul until I allowed Him to restore my reason.

That's what He does for His children, if we'll only let Him. But guess what? The truth is that even when I was in the depths of my discouragement, God covered me with His grace.

A TV interviewer asked Martha Williamson, executive producer of *Touched by an Angel,* what the message of her show was. She replied, "God loves you; deal with it!"

My discouragement didn't put off God. I might have been ready to give up on me, but He wasn't. I am His beloved daughter. Having heard my every heartbeat from my mother's womb to my current point of despair, He wasn't about to abandon me. He didn't quit with the first dirty diaper or the all-night bout with colic. God had invested too much of Himself to give up now.

My Father looked beyond my grief and fear and continued to love me. He ignored my kicking and screaming, my tantrums, and my angry and hate-filled words. God looked beyond my turmoil into my heart of hearts, the secret place of which the psalmist speaks, to my innermost being and read my true desires.

I began to heal. However, like a kid who scrapes her knees, then picks at the scabs with her dirty hands, I would reopen my wounds, causing new infections. Yet God's healing process continued. I discovered that just as praise is a choice, so is discouragement. And discouragement leads to depression, and depression to death.

Before long I looked toward Him instead of toward myself. My courage grew. He told me that to heal completely, I must share with others what He'd done for me. That was difficult to do. Now that my reason had been restored, I didn't really want people to know that the confident, joyous woman standing in front of them had once considered committing suicide. How embarrassing!

Patiently, lovingly, my heavenly Father reminded me that living with "no fear" means just that, no fear—underlined and capitalized in bold type. "Kay," He said, "don't be afraid what people will think of you for sharing your weak moment with them. Instead, rejoice at what they will learn about Me through what I've done through you."

My reason for being is to glorify God. It is in bringing honor and praise to His holy name that I maintain my residence in His kingdom.

I am told that when one backpacks into the High Sierras, it is important not to camp below the snake line. In the Alpine region the air is thin and the flora sparse. Snakes and other such creatures can't stand the frigid temperatures of the upper mountain regions. I must admit that if I were camping in snake-infested terrain, I'd want to keep hiking until I crossed that invisible snake line too. Somehow it doesn't cheer me to imagine crawling into my sleeping bag and discovering I'm not alone, that a wood rattler is seeking warmth.

As children of God who rightly qualify to reside in God's

kingdom, it makes no sense to go camping beneath the snake line on Satan's ground of fear, complaint, and despair.

Ellen White wrote in *My Life Today:* "Heaven is full of joy. It resounds with the praise of Him who made so wonderful a sacrifice for the redemption of the human race. . . . Those who in heaven join with the angelic choir in their anthem of praise must learn on earth the song of heaven, the keynote of which is thanksgiving" (p. 359).

Six

My Will for Him

"In everything give thanks: for this is the will of God in Christ Jesus concerning you."
—1 Thessalonians 5:18, KJV

I n the sentence "I will praise You" the operative word is *will*. I choose to praise my God, because He has said to do so more than 350 times in His Word. I elect to praise my Father, because praise is the identifying feature of His chosen people (1 Peter 2:9). Praise is my ID card. Just as my California driver's license identifies me by photo and signature as Kay D. Rizzo, so my attitude of praise reveals that I am a daughter of the heavenly King. Wherever I go, people will know that I am my Father's girl through my genuine praise.

Other Bible authors refer to praise as a protective hedge or as defensive armor. Psalm 103:1-5 lists the benefits that become mine when I praise Him. Operating from a paradigm of praise changes everything.

I love to visit a fun house, a place where smoke and mirrors and optical illusions confuse reality. For a few minutes it is exciting, but it is not a place where I'd want to spend the rest of my life. Unfortunately, the father of lies has convinced many people that the here-and-now world of muck and mayhem is the only reality and that heaven is a fantasy or an illusion. In actuality, the permanence of this world is the illusion and heaven is the ultimate reality.

Satan would have me believe that right is wrong, good is bad, and that the truly bad is enjoyable. One evening I was watching a film in which a couple married to other partners struggled to get together. It took a commercial for me to stop and realize that I'd been rooting for the adulterous pair. The realization horrified me. For a brief moment I had allowed my earthly experience to over-shadow the reality that God is God and that human arrogance and lust can lead only to disaster.

Just when I think I have all the answers, someone changes the questions. The realities of this world—all the human "truths"— are upside down and inside out to the reality of God's kingdom. The longer I live in Jesus, the more I discover how erroneous my personal beliefs and opinions are. Like the apostle Paul, I'm learning to distrust my own opinions and motives and wait for God to make His will and His reality known to me. Surrendering my highly developed notions along with my will to Him and to the reality of His will is not always easy.

"When God draws me, the issue of my will comes in at once. . . . If I will, I shall find I am based on Reality that is as sure as God's throne. . . . There must be a surrender of the will, not a surrender to persuasive power, a deliberate launching forth on God and on what He says until I am no longer confident in what I have done, I am confident only in God. . . . This can never be done without a violent effort on my part to disassociate myself from my old ways of looking at things" (Oswald Chambers, *My Utmost for His Highest*, pp. 265, 266).

I enjoy having my own way. While I may acquiesce to please others so that they will like me, I much prefer doing things my way. If I want a piece of chocolate fudge, don't try to give me a vanilla caramel instead. Or if I think I need a new purse, don't tell me I can't have it just because I don't have any cash in hand. I'll charge it. The battle of wills isn't won or lost on plastic or at the candy counter or with any other problem I face in the external world. For me, the battle is won or lost in the secret places of my will.

— 55 —

"Nothing has any power over the man who has fought out the battle [of the will] before God and won there" (*ibid.*, p. 269). Notice that Chambers didn't say that the battle of the will is with God, but "before God." The victory is mine when I choose to turn over my will to Him.

"It is not a question of giving up sin, but of giving up my right to myself, my natural independence and self-assertiveness, and this is where the battle has to be fought" (*ibid.*, p. 256).

When I chose to become a child of God, my rights became His as well. Such a transaction of my will is not a natural course for me, but a divine action. My intellect shouts, "Don't be a fool! Look out for number one! Stay in control of your destiny." Sometimes my emotions whine and complain about my great sacrifice.

I've heard sermons about the tremendus sacrifices we make for our Lord and I laugh. What sacrifices? Oh dear, must I give up the right to booze my liver into collapse? I will never be arrested for shoplifting or thrown into prison for murder? I won't be lonely or despondent again? Sacrifices?

A friend sent me a quote from an article by Catherine Marshall in which Mrs. Marshall tells about a conversation she had with God at a particularly low point in her life. She'd been reading 1 Thessalonians 5:18: "In everything give thanks: for this is the will of God in Christ Jesus concerning you" (KJV).

She prayed about the text. "You mean that even in the midst of difficult or tragic circumstances, by an act of will, I'm to thank You? Isn't that almost hypocritical?"

God answered, "Obedience means turning your back on your problem or the grief and directing your eyes and attention toward Me. Then I will supply the emotion to make the praise real." It is one of the greatest benefits I've gained from praise—the conversion of my negative thoughts into positive energy.

Morton Kelsey wrote in his book *Healing and Christianity* (New York: Harper and Row, 1973) that "the brain and the immune system make up a closed circuit. Drawing on the most sophisticated techniques of psychology, neurobiology, and immunology, research shows that the brain can enhance or inhibit the body's defenses. . . . Signals from the immune system also reach rational and emotional centers of the brain, which may explain why people become irritable when they're sick, and why mental capacity often deteriorates at the same time as resistance to infection.

"Since these pathways are affected by thoughts and emotions, it is not surprising that mental states can alter the course of an illness. Research shows that people who perceive a lack of control in their lives, who feel helpless, demonstrate significantly reduced activity of the natural killer cells, or white blood cells, in their immune system" (p. 219).

Jean Achterberg observes that "no thought, no emotion is without biochemical, electrochemical activity; the activity leaves no cell untouched" (*Imagery in Healing* [Boston: New Science Library, 1985], p. 5).

Negative thinking is expensive. Dragging us down mentally, emotionally, and physically, it is a luxury the child of God cannot afford.

Peter McWilliams, the coauthor of *You Can't Afford the Luxury of One Negative Thought,* says, "Worrying is a form of atheism."

The cure for the disease of negative thinking is to align our will with that of the Father, or praising God. And the reward is eternal life—not a ho-hum lifestyle, but life to its utmost! Instead of the woes of defeat, I can hear the sounds of creation and re-creation humming within my own body. I can have an eternity of health and happiness for the price of simple obedience!

Did you get that? Just as frosting adds to the enjoyment of a slice of cake, so God adds joy, health, and healing to our obedience—the emotional frosting that is ours from submitting to God's perfect will. By setting my mind "on things above" (Col. 3:2) through my praise, "the things of earth . . . grow strangely dim in the light of His glory and grace."

A few weeks ago a woman asked me, "How do you know you are living in God's will? I think I am, but I don't feel a thing."

My answer had to be: "What do feelings have to do with it? We're dealing with God's promises here, not our response. We're talking faith here. Faith doesn't wait around for the feelings to set in. It's never safe to let our feelings guide us. Feeling can be affected by too many outside influences, not the least being habits, demons, and misconceptions." I pointed to my head. "Obedience happens first up here before in here." Then I indicated my heart. "If after you obey, you receive an emotional response, great. If not, so what? God is God, and His Word is sure."

A friend once asked, "How does your praise thing differ from the popular power of positive thinking—'If I think it, I can make it so'?"

First of all, praise is not my thing—it's God's. Next, I am sure that thinking positively will never hurt anyone, but praise goes beyond just a determination to shed negative thoughts. Positive thinking works to a point, but like anything else we try to do for ourselves, it will break down eventually. We can't manufacture our own strength. It comes from an unlimited source—God.

Stories out of prison camps show that those who survived were the ones who focused on God. They quoted Scripture, sang hymns of praise, prayed, talked of hope, and aided and encouraged other prisoners. The ingredient for survival was the focus of their positive attitude, God—not the attitude itself.

Remember the "balancing the broom" game you played as a kid? You placed the end of the broom handle in the palm of your flattened hand and tried to balance the broom. The only way you could keep the broom from falling was to lift your eyes away from the point where the broom touched your hand (the problem area) to the top of the broom. Only then could you balance it. Praising lifts our eyes from our problems and focuses our attention onto our God. That God's will is for us to praise Him is for our sakes more than His.

The Greek word for mind, *dianoi,* means "thinking through, meditating, reflecting, the faculty of moral reflection." Here is the part that Romans 12:2 says must be renewed.

Theologian J. Oswald Sanders wrote: "We must learn to live in the region of the will, not in the changeful realm of feelings. It is what we choose, not what we feel, that is important" (*Cultivation of Christian Character*, p. 29).

Seven

The Word and the Will

"The world and its desires pass away, but the man who does the will of God lives forever."
—1 John 2:17

H ardly a day passes that I don't see or feel a new sign of aging coming on. I remember my mother saying before her death at 88, "Old age isn't for sissies." She was anything but a sissy. Her life had spanned the horse-and-buggy age, the golden age of train travel, and then jets and spaceships. Even after the age of 80 she crisscrossed the continent several times to see grandchildren and great-grandchildren. She broke the taboos of her era by wearing pantsuits (I never could convince her to try blue jeans), and her bland English tastebuds grew to enjoy Mexican, Italian, and Greek foods as well. But alas, her body wore out like a much-loved winter coat. Today she's resting in her Saviour's promise of restoration. One of her favorite sayings was "God willing." She tagged every plan she made for tomorrow with "God willing." At times it irked me, but I've come to understand the purpose and the theology of that phrase.

My affections remain firm in God's perfect will when I choose to renew my mind as described in Romans 12:2. It is God's will that I study His Word. For years I found such study boring, especially when I tried to meet specific guidelines for "good" Bible study. When I discovered the individuality of praise in my worship, I realized that just as God made each of us unique and one of a kind, our worship of Him will be just as individual and special.

I read a lot about cloning these days, of making one creature an exact replica of another. Somehow I don't think that's the Creator's plan for His kids. Will He allow humanity to manipulate the genes enough to create ourselves as we wish? I don't know. For years my mother never believed human beings would walk on the moon's surface, but they did. Whether or not genetic research will be able to design a line of cookie-cutter Christians or stamp out an exclusive line of Barbie Doll confections before God turns such attempts into Babel is unimportant. Nothing will change the fact that I am unique. I am me.

Unfortunately, my sin problem is not unique. And the cure is uniform as well—Jesus Christ alone and His sacrifice for me. Therefore, my worship must be focused on Him. It is part of my spiritual exercise program.

As any physical fitness guru will tell you, an exercise program must reflect the individual's personality and lifestyle. The secret to success is to find your style of exercise and, as Nike says, "just do it!"

Personal worship is similar. Recently I read a book called *Sacred Pathways*. The author described seven personalities and their unique worship patterns, using characters from the Bible to illustrate the different worshipers and styles of worship. A sanguine personality like mine may enjoy the energy and vitality received from a rousing praise service, while a melancholy personality would appreciate more the tradition and splendor of high church.

So my personal worship tastes may differ from my sister's as well. I like spending quiet time on my patio in the morning before I take my daily walk or swim. Also I enjoy meditating on a passage from the book of Philippians or from 1 John or Psalms. A word or a phrase might trigger my curiosity and send me delving into its etymology. And that's OK.

My melancholy friend might prefer an organized study of God's Word. She likes being able to check off the chapters she reads. It feeds her need to see results. And that's OK too.

As long as my daily worship contains prayer and praise to my Creator—my part of the dialogue—along with study and meditation on His Words to me—His part of the bargain—then I will grow strong spiritually. It's the routine, the practice, that makes the difference, not the sameness.

When my elder daughter, Rhonda, began playing the piano, she, like most children, hit a few sour notes. But as she practiced she became proficient, until in time she mastered the keyboard. Today she is a concert pianist. Yet even at this level of performance, Rhonda realizes she will always have more to learn. So God's Word grows more and more enjoyable each day, and no matter how knowledgeable I may become, there will always be more to learn.

Training is like that, whether in sports, music, or spiritual development. Peace, joy, and love grow in the submissive heart as naturally as carrot seeds and lima beans sprout in carefully prepared soil. My praise makes my heart submissive. It puts me in the proper perspective with my heavenly Father. As my heavenly Father, He deserves my honor.

Richard and I were halfway through our dinner when Chucky and his entourage chose to eat at a table a few feet from ours. At first glance we knew the 3-year-old with the springy blond curls, dimpled chin, and sparkling blue eyes reigned over his fawning subjects, who appeared to be his parents and his grandmother. When the older woman wandered toward a booth near the window, the little boy whined, "I want to sit over here!"

The grandmother and the boy's mother exchanged glances, then acquiesced to the child's demands. It caused my husband and me to exchange glances as well.

The battle of wills continued while they waited to order their meal. Chucky didn't want to sit in a high chair. He preferred a bolster chair. Then when everyone was settled, he announced his desire to sit by Daddy instead of Mommy. A grim game of musical chairs followed.

Ordering triggered a tussle between the mother and the boy. Chucky demanded a strawberry ice-cream sundae. He got a strawberry ice-cream sundae. "Milk and fruit are good for him," the father drooled.

Throughout the meal the child either whined or wailed until the three adults gave in and let him eat from their plates. When the older woman resisted, the child's mother explained, "Chucky can be so unpleasant when crossed."

Richard and I watched in disbelief as the boy turned the area around his table into a toxic waste disposal site. Any attempt to control him resulted in wails worthy of a top-of-the-line police siren.

When Chucky had eaten as much as he pleased from his and his family's plates, he slid off his chair and headed for the meals of other diners. I eyed the grinning Chucky as he sidled up to our table and peered into my face. We smiled at each other. Slowly his chubby little hand crept over the edge of my dessert plate.

"No!" I moved my chocolate-chip cookie out of his reach. He tried a second time. This time I wagged a finger in front of his face. "I said no! Don't even think about it!"

My stern voice surprised the child. His eyes widened with fear. Snatching back his hand, he turned away from our table. I hadn't intended to eat the cookie, but I certainly wasn't going to allow Chucky the pleasure of helping himself to it.

My high school science teacher of a husband growled as we left the restaurant, "I'm glad I'll be retired before he registers for any of my classes."

I agreed, saddened as I thought of the beautiful but already petulant face of that little boy. If the pattern continued, happiness, like my cookie, would always be just out of his reach. His tirades would become destructive.

Proverbs says to "train up a child in the way he should go" (Prov. 22:6, KJV). A wise parent knows that he or she must be in control of the situation. Children whose wills are not bent into obedience grow up with a false view of society. They do not learn to respect authority. Everything is their way or no way. It can be a trial for new parents, finding the balance between harmful indulgence of a child and unreasonable oppression.

So it is in the second birth. We must learn proper respect for the Father, Son, and Holy Spirit. And as with a young child, respect is a battle of wills.

When Jesus appeared on earth to provide us with an example, He said He had come to do "the will of him who sent me" (John 6:38). In Gethsemane, when His humanity cried out for an escape, He said, "Not my will, but thine, be done" (Luke 22:42, KJV). Even under such extreme circumstances, He chose to align His will with that of His Father's.

Jesus warned His disciples, "Not everyone who says to me, 'Lord, Lord,' will enter the kingdom of heaven, but only he who does the will of my Father'" (Matt. 7:21).

What is the Father's will?

"What if He wants me to dedicate my life to the lepers of India or to wash the feet of Los Angeles' indigent population?" you ask.

I would answer, "So?" We never need to be afraid of God's plans for us. God will not lead you where His grace cannot keep you. Romans 8:15 declares: "For you did not receive a spirit that makes you a slave again to fear, but you received the Spirit of sonship. And by him we cry, 'Abba, Father.'"

God is a good Father. He will never purposely harm His sons and daughters, but He will place them where they can shine as His kids.

Recently Kelli took my grandson to the doctor for his monthly shots, not because she hated him or wanted to punish him for not napping for as long as she might have liked, but because she loves him and knows the shots will protect him from far more serious pain. Likewise God inoculates us at times, not as a punishment but because He loves us.

The Holy Spirit Himself testifies that we are God's children, hence heirs to the kingdom. The kingdom of God is among you if you live in the atmosphere of His will.

And if we believe our Father to be a God of love, we must also believe that God will never lead us where His grace cannot keep us. What a concept of faith. I like that, don't you? David asked, in Psalm 143:10, "Teach me to do your will, for you are my God." Philippians 2:13 says: "It is God who works in you to will and to act according to his good purpose." The author of Hebrews also says that the "great Shepherd of the sheep" equips you "with everything good for doing his will" (Heb. 13:20, 21).

Promises in both Psalms and Ezekiel tell me that God will give me a new heart and a new spirit in order to live by His will.

My first step was to recognize my need for the Saviour. Jesus didn't say "I'll show you the way" or "I'll give you a road map" or "I'll tell you which way to go." Instead He declared, "I am the Way."

Along with recognizing my need for the redeeming love of Jesus in my life, I confess my sins. "To confess" is one of the definitions of praise. We are never closer to our Saviour than when we come face-to-face with Him to ask for His forgiveness. The forgiveness of sin is the reason He died for us.

Here are just a few texts regarding God's will for each of us:

That He wants to renew our minds with His Word: "his good, pleasing and perfect will" (Rom. 12:2).

That we should have praise and thanksgiving: "Give thanks in all circumstances, for this is God's will" (1 Thess. 5:18).

That we should be sanctified: "It is God's will that you should be sanctified" (1 Thess. 4:3). And He will do the sanctifying.

Scholars and theologians debate the process, diagram their

theories, and couch their findings in eloquent terms when the truth is, in Jesus' words, "My yoke is easy and my burden is light."

A good illustration on giving the will over to God might appear in the story of the Sunday school picnic and the bologna sandwich. Johnny heard the announcement at church one week regarding the afternoon Sunday school picnic. After church he hurried home to make a lunch to take to the picnic. All he could find was two stale slices of bread, a piece of dried-up bologna, and barely enough mustard to spread on one slice of bread.

At the picnic one of his friends invited him to sit with his family for the meal. Johnny almost drooled as he watched his friend's mother open the giant picnic basket and removed a huge container of potato salad, a tub of fried chicken, coleslaw, pickles, olives, a pot of baked beans, a jug of lemonade, and a triple-decker chocolate cake.

Trying to be inconspicuous, the boy unwrapped his bologna sandwich. "Johnny," his friend's mother asked, "why don't you add your food to ours? We'll have a potluck. Besides, I sure do like bologna sandwiches."

Johnny tried to resist, but the woman broke down his reserve by waving a juicy chicken leg in front of his face. What an exchange! Whether his friend's mother ever ate the bologna sandwich I don't know, but I do know Johnny didn't leave the table hungry.

Don't get lost in a debate over the woman's Southern fried chicken or the bologna in the sandwich. The story isn't about meat-eating, but about the woman's generous offer.

Johnny would have been a fool (and a hungry one, at that) to turn down his friend's mother's offer. So the child of God would be a fool to cling to his or her dried-up, brown-tinged bologna sandwich when he or she can have a banquet of delights instead. When I turn over my will to my Father, all of heaven's delights are mine. And all I have to sacrifice is one aging bologna sandwich. Johnny didn't leave the picnic table hungry that day—and neither do I when I release my will and accept God's abundance as mine.

Eight

The Dialect of Praise

"I will bow down toward your holy temple and will praise your name for your love and your faithfulness."
— Psalm 138:2

In college, when I needed to learn a second language in order to graduate, I chose French. In my imagination I could hear myself rattling off with ease those beautiful-sounding phrases. "Monsieur Le Beurre"—sounds romantic, doesn't it? Of course, I seldom call anyone Mr. Butter, but it sounds lovely regardless.

Two years of French later, I was far from making the French language mine. I could read and translate—sort of. Or I could listen to someone speaking French and pick out familiar phrases—more or less. And I thought I had a fairly decent speaking vocabulary until my husband, my two daughters, and I toured Quebec on a summer vacation.

When we crossed the U.S. border, I was delighted to discover that I could interpret road signs and advertisements along the way. Of course, Coca-Cola is identifiable in any language. However, I had no intention of speaking the language to anyone French—until we arrived in a small town in northern Quebec. The town resembled a set from the old American West, un-painted storefronts, wooden sidewalks, and all. We pulled our Chevy station wagon and tent trailer to a stop beside the rustic

— 68 —

sidewalk where two young boys were playing marbles. *How quaint,* I thought. I hadn't seen kids play marbles in many years. This looked like a safe place to try out my speaking skills. I called out to the boys, "Bonjour." *So far, so good,* I thought.

The boys squinted over at me where I stood beside our car. Then I asked, or thought I asked, "Could you please tell me where I might find a pharmacy?"

The two boys' eyes widened, then they shrieked with laughter and ran inside the nearest building, undoubtedly to tell some adult about the crazy Yankee and her hapless attempt to speak the French language. To this day I don't know what I said, but whatever it was, it surely touched their funny bones. From then on I decided to relegate my limited knowledge of the French language to the presence of family members only.

If I wanted to become proficient at speaking French, I would need to learn a whole lot more than I knew at present. As a friend once told me, you know your second language when you begin to dream in it. I was far from dreaming in French.

It was the same for Italian. When Richard and I visited his mother's home on Sabbath, guests would pack their warm, comfortable kitchen, where we clustered around the large maple table, eating lasagna, cracking pistachio nuts, and talking through long summer afternoons. Since most of those present spoke Italian as well as English, it wasn't unusual for a person to be speaking in English and switch to Italian, then back to English, before reaching the end of their sentence, using whichever language best expressed their thoughts. Everyone but my husband and me followed the shift. It drove Richard crazy, since he'd never learned his ancestral language as a child. I didn't fare much better, being of English-Scottish descent. Despite my best efforts to follow the conversation, I failed because I didn't know the Italian language and I didn't ask anyone to interpret for me.

Those conversations were to me much like the child of God's praising must sound to the "unconditioned" ear. Before I discovered this new and exciting dialect, I would hear people praise God and think, *Cliché! Nothing new here!*

An old man couldn't stop praising God. Several times during every sermon the old man would interrupt the preacher with exclamations of "Praise God!" It seemed as if no matter what the preacher spoke about, the man would interrupt with the familiar phrase.

One Sunday, in desperation, the preacher placed the old man in a room behind the sanctuary with a copy of the *National Geographic* magazine. In the middle of the Sunday sermon the preacher heard the old man bellow from the other room, "Praise God!"

After the service the preacher asked the man what he'd possibly found in a copy of *National Geographic* that he could praise God about. The old man pointed to a paragraph about the Mariana Islands in the South Pacific. "It says here, Pastor, that the deepest part of the ocean is more than seven miles deep. That's where my sins are buried! Praise God!"

I remember laughing indulgently at the old man's wisdom, but it wasn't until I began speaking the language of heaven that I could comprehend what he had discovered. The more I praise, the more I find to praise. The language needed to become my own.

Dreaming in praise—that's a possibility too. When I go to sleep praising, I awaken in the morning where my praises left off the night before. For several years I dreamed a certain bad dream. I'd wake up sobbing and despondent. Since I began practicing the dialect of praise, the disturbing dream returns less and less frequently.

Several years ago Richard took up ham radio. He had to learn Morse code in order to acquire his radio license. He practiced it day and night, tapping out letters with his fork at the dinner table and with his fingers while watching the evening news. One night soon after he received his ham operator's license in the mail, we were sleeping when suddenly Richard sat bolt upright in bed.

"Listen!" he whispered. "Did you hear that?"

Bleary-eyed from sleep, I mumbled, "Hear what?"

"That! Did you hear that? Listen!"

"What? I don't hear anything. Go back to sleep." I rolled over and slipped back into my slumber. I don't know how much time passed before Richard hissed, "There it is! Didn't you hear it?"

"No," I muttered into my pillow. "I didn't hear anything."

"Honey, I think someone's in trouble."

"What?"

"Someone's in trouble. I can hear him tapping out a signal for help in Morse code."

Sighing, I squinted at the glowing numbers on the face of the clock. "Richard, it's 4:00 in the morning! No one's calling for help at this hour."

He lay back down and adjusted the blankets under his chin. "You're probably right. Who would be out there at this hour?"

I'd barely returned to my dream state when my husband leaped out of bed. "Kay, I know what I hear. And I hear someone tapping out a plea for help. I've got to go see who it is."

He hauled on his trousers, shirt, socks, and shoes, grabbed his jacket from the hall closet, and disappeared out the front door. Reluctantly I dragged myself out of bed. As I was putting on my robe I too heard the tapping. It wasn't a figment of my husband's imagination. It was real. And even with my limited knowledge of Morse code, it sounded like the letters S-O-S.

Before I could slip my feet into my flip-flops, I heard what seemed like someone pawing around our bedroom window. I ran to my daughters' rooms to be certain they were OK. Both were sleeping soundly. Next I hurried to the front door and called, "Richard? Richard?"

A shadowy form emerged from around the corner of the garage. I peered into the night. "Richard? Is that you?"

"Yeah, it's only me." He climbed the front steps to where I stood. "It's nothing. Go back to bed." He brushed past me into the warmth of our parlor.

"What do you mean it's nothing? I heard it too. Maybe there's been a car crash down on the highway and the injured driver has crawled up here to get help."

"Naw, it's really nothing." He shed his coat and took a drink from the kitchen faucet.

"It wasn't nothing—I know I heard something."

Turning toward me, he mumbled, "It was only a branch tapping our bedroom window."

"What?" I started to giggle.

"The wind was blowing the branch against the windowpane. It just happened to be in the S-O-S sequence." He reddened. "I broke it off so it couldn't do it any longer."

To this day I tease Richard about the branch's unique interpretation of the Morse code. To me the tapping meant nothing. To my husband's trained ear, it was a message. Even now, at the sound of dots and dashes, Richard pauses whatever he's doing to listen.

As with the Morse code, praise is an entirely new language, along with a new way of thinking. Now that I'm familiar with the dialect, I hear it spoken everywhere I turn. I read it everywhere I look. And I find myself inserting it wherever it is appropriate. "My tongue will sing of your righteousness. O Lord, open my lips, and my mouth will declare your praise" (Ps. 51:14, 15).

Praise is more than repeating the same words again and again, though there have been times during intimate communion with the Father that this repetitive form of worship has been effective for me.

Don't get hung up with the word "repetitive." A great difference exists between the word "repetition" and the phrase "vain repetition." *Roget's Thesaurus* defines "vain" as "futile, boastful, hopeless, ineffective, proud, self-important, and baseless," none of which apply to the praise I give my Father.

Praise is infinitely more than some ponderous Shakespearean soliloquy delivered in sacred tones. An attitude of praise allows me to glorify Him with the abandon of a little child in rhyme, in verse, in laughter, or in song.

The dialect of praise is a language of love. Praise involves sharing one's whole self. When Jesus tells us that we must know Him (see Matt. 7:23), He uses the same word often found in the Old Testament for sexual union. It may make some people uncomfortable, but one of the definitions for praise, or *halel* in Hebrew, is "intense worship."

"God calls us into a mystical union that is intimate, passionate and involves the totality of who we are. New Testament writers use the symbolism of the bride and bridegroom to describe the union between Christ and the church—us" (Kenneth Bakken and Kathleen H. Hofeller, *The Journey Toward Wholeness: A Christ Centered Approach to Health and Healing* [New York: Crossroads, 1988]). The dialect of praise is also the language of life.

Recently I read a free verse poem titled "A Lifetime of Dying." It goes like this:

"As a child, I was dying to go to school
And then I was dying to get into high school
And then I was dying to get my driver's license
And then I was dying to go to college
And then I was dying to graduate college
And then I was dying to marry and have children
And then I was dying for the children to grow up
   so I could go to work
And then I was dying to retire
And suddenly I was dying
And I realized I'd spent so much time dying that
   I'd forgotten to live."

Scary, isn't it? But all too true. Too often we wish our lives away. I'm guilty of doing it too. Next week I'll have enough money for my new jacket. Next month we can pay off our car loan. Next summer we'll visit the kids in Portland. Next year we'll . . . I'm sure you get the picture. And perhaps you can see yourself in it as well.

Learning to speak the dialect of praise teaches me to stop and collect the lilacs from the bushes beside the highway. It directs my gaze toward the edelweiss scattered over the most rocky of mountainsides. Praise encourages me to abandon my computer screen long enough to laugh at a sparrow on my patio stealing kibbles from our dog's dish. And it reminds me not to rush through the good times but to seek God's signature in every event in my life.

A favorite author of mine wrote, "Those who enter heaven must learn on earth the song of heaven, the keynote of which is praise and thanksgiving. Only as they learn this song can they join in singing it with the heavenly choir" (Ellen G. White, in *Atlantic Union Gleaner*, Aug. 20, 1902).

When I was a little girl I thought my daddy was the wisest, the strongest, the greatest father that ever lived. I had no trouble praising him. But alas, I grew older and "wiser." I noticed that my friend Ann's father sometimes preached when our minister was out of town. Mine never did that. For that matter, I never saw my father speak in front of an audience. Now, I knew that people who spoke from the pulpit were ready for translation. Maybe my dad wasn't so perfect after all.

Also I began to notice as I "matured" that my father, a painting contractor, came to church with paint in the creases of his knuckles. I watched him scrub his hands with strong chemicals to remove the paint, but traces of paint remained. My father's "dirty" hands embarrassed me. In my "maturity" I wasn't as mature as I thought. I still hadn't made the connection between the paint on my father's hands with the poodle skirt in my closet or with the petal pink sweater set in my bureau drawer. And I still didn't really know my father.

As the years passed I became less concerned with the traces of paint visible in the wrinkles of my dad's hands and more with his limited wardrobe. He had a red corduroy shirt that he wore everywhere—to the grocery store, to prayer meeting, to job estimates—everywhere! In my burgeoning fashion-conscious mind I wished he'd wear snappy sport shirts like those worn by the fathers of my friends. And I wished he'd throw away those ugly fat ties he wore to church on Sabbath with his suit and buy a couple sleek narrow ties that were all the rage. And his shoes! Plain brown oxfords!

It took a long time for me to grow up enough to rediscover the daddy I'd known as a little child, to recognize him for the gentlest, most gracious and loving dad a girl could have. My myopic vision had missed so much for so many years.

His legacy of generosity lives in the lives of hundreds of young people whom he helped to acquire a Christian education, including me. When it came to raising funds for church-sponsored activities, he was there, checkbook in hand. Or when the church steeple needed painting, he showed up with brush, paint can, and ladder. At Ingathering time—try to keep up with him!

And faithful? Never was there a man so faithful as my dad. No matter how low the Northeastern temperatures may have dropped the night before, the church auditorium was toasty warm when the rest of the members arrived for the morning services. I remember when one of the presidents from our local church conference joked from the pulpit that "Norman Hancock is the only man who ever beat me to church on Sabbath morning."

I remember those Sabbath mornings too. I couldn't for the life of me understand why we had to be up and ready for church by 8:00 a.m. when church didn't start until 9:15, especially since it was less than 15 minutes away from our home. When I asked, he'd say, "People depend on me, Kay. When someone's depending on you, you don't let them down."

Once my dad and I were painting the kitchen. My job was to

paint inside the cupboards. Grumbling, I set about my task. I couldn't understand why the inside of the cupboards had to be painted anyway. When I reached the sink, I asked if I had to paint behind the pipes as well. My dad said I did. Groaning, I mumbled, "If I didn't paint there, no one would ever know."

He paused with paintbrush in hand. "You would and I would, and that's what's important."

Today I remember my dad as the kind of father who exemplified so many God-traits. I needed to mature before I could see him once again through the unaffected eyes of a little child.

My pattern with God was similar in nature. As a tiny child, lisping the name of Jesus, I gazed at Him in wonder. But as I "matured" I observed what I interpreted as chinks in His armor. In my newly acquired wisdom, I asked, "Why does God allow this? And why did that happen?"

The dialect of praise took me full circle to where I could view my heavenly Father again through the eyes of a child, to where I could once again appreciate Him for who He is—my Father and my God.

Nine

Seeking God

"Let the hearts of those who seek the Lord rejoice."
—Psalm 105:3

ike most proud mothers, my mother loved to regale people with humorous stories about her children's past, much to the pain of the child involved. The following is one of those stories. When I was a child of 3 or so, I wanted to play hide-and-seek with my 12-year-old sister, Connie, and her friends. Connie wasn't too excited about having her 3-year-old sister tagging after her in a high-energy game such as hide-and-seek. But Mama prevailed, and I was allowed to play with the big kids.

Reluctantly they let me be "it." Following their earlier example, I buried my face against the trunk of our backyard maple tree, then proceeded to count. "Yi-yi-yi-yi-yi-yi-yi! Ready or not, here I come!"

That was my first encounter with hide-and-seek. And only a mother would find it the least bit amusing. However, I remember another game of hide-and-seek when I was much older that wasn't so cute. I'd found a great hiding place. I waited and waited for my friends to find me, but no one did. After what seemed like hours to my young brain, I slipped out of my hiding place and discovered that my friends had abandoned me and the game for Popsicles. The instant that one of the mothers on the block announced Popsicles for everyone, they forgot me.

I am so glad that God doesn't play hide-and-seek with me. And I am even more thankful that God and His promises are visible to me. He isn't into game playing, but assures us that all who seek Him with their whole hearts will always find Him.

Religion, despite the fact that we must do something about our relationship with God, can become bad news if it traps us in a game that we will always and everywhere lose. But the good news is that through the death and resurrection of Jesus Christ, God has called off the game. He's taken all the disasters that religion tries to remedy and sets them right. His church must no longer be in the religion business, but in the gospel-proclaiming business. Creed, cult, or conduct are no longer the touchstones of salvation. The good news is that Christ died so that I may seek God without the aid of a blue-nosed bookkeeper or a scorecard. Instead He actively lures me to His side through the gentle whisper of the Holy Spirit—no mystery, no intrigue, just genuine love. And when I seek Him in love, He promises to be found.

I must leave my personal agendas behind if I truly wish to see God. My purpose for seeking Him must be more than a fire escape or for help getting out of one scrape or another. And I must admit that through the years I've sought God for my own selfish reasons more often than only for the pleasure of seeing God as He really is.

Despite my selfish motives, God has been patient with me. He's answered my prayers regardless of my motives. For that I am grateful. But because of my shallow approach to God I had a shallow view of Him as well. I didn't really know Him. That is where praise changed everything.

Praise creates in me a new hunger and thirst for knowing God—really knowing Him. When my praise puts me in the right perspective with my Father, when I am no longer the focus of my own attention, I see facets of my God that I'd previously missed, and they fill me with awe.

I have the privilege of traveling around the country, sharing my praise experience with all kinds of people. Lest you think all this travel is joyous and light, every now and then it isn't.

After fighting wind, rain, and messed-up travel connections, I, the keynote speaker for a weekend women's retreat, finally arrived at the vacation resort where it was being held. It was after midnight when I unlocked the door to my room. While the cramped, dark, and scruffy room might have been decorated in an earlier era, it lacked that era's charm.

On checking the bathroom, I discovered that the tub had so many rings I began calling it Saturn. The mirrors were smudged with fingerprints, hair spray, and noseprints (yes, I examined them closely!). The telephone receiver was so corroded with grime that I washed it with soap and water before I held it to my ear to call home.

Having traveled several hours that day, I was tired, miserable, and wet from dragging my luggage through monsoon rains. My throat, ears, and nose warned me that I was coming down with a flu bug. All I wanted to do was wash the grime off my face, but the bathroom had no facecloths. I called housekeeping, but could get no response.

I was handling it all pretty well until the desk clerk told me that the conference committee members were ensconced in spacious, newly decorated suites, some with in-room hot tubs! Hot tubs! Every muscle in my body screamed for justice. I felt absolutely mistreated and abandoned.

Sitting in the middle of my hard lumpy bed and picking at a poorly repaired patch in the 1960s-print bedspread, I felt sorry for myself. Tears rolled down my fevered cheeks. "I wanna go home," I wailed, causing my already pounding headache to shift into overdrive.

Within a few minutes my wailing turned to laughter when I

remembered my daughter Kelli's adventure in India. Missionaries with Celebrant Singers, she and her husband, Mark, arrived at a primitive youth camp. The tiny room to which they were assigned crawled with vermin of every kind, including spiders, ants, cockroaches, and rats. The sheets on the bed were so encrusted with dirt, that chunks of it, like plaster on a drop cloth, broke off when you turned them back. The smell of sweat and human waste nauseated her.

Exhausted from the long trip and homesick, she had sat in the middle of the bed and cried, "This is all a mistake. I wasn't meant to be a missionary, God. I want to go home!"

Kelli survived the cockroaches, the filthy sheets, and a whole lot worse before she returned home, including three days in a hospital on IVs. Along with the discomfort, she discovered a very real joy in sharing her God with people in an area where "His light is dim and His voice is heard small."

Despite my surroundings, my little hotel room filled with laughter. At least I had running water, and I didn't have to use a contraption called a "squatty potty."

When my reason returned, I heard God remind me, "Kay, someone had to sleep in this room. The hotel is full. So many hungry sisters are here for a blessing, a blessing of which you will be a part. Are you any better than your sisters?

"So a few have hot tubs and you don't—so what? Did I ever promise you a hot tub? What I did promise was 'Never will I leave you; never will I forsake you.'

"So even if the tub you received resembles the planet Saturn, it has hot and cold running water—that's more than King Solomon enjoyed in all his splendor. So your mirror would be a great advertisement for the power of Windex cleaner, so your telephone receiver is coated with the earwax of a hundred somebodies, you can still dial (and I do mean dial) home and hear your husband's voice. So you have the flu and the room feels like an overheated crypt, it could be cold and damp and musty smelling. I promised that I will never leave you, that I will never forsake you."

Then He reminded me of Pastor Noble Alexander, who'd spent 22 years in a Cuban prison for preaching the gospel of Jesus Christ. I preached the gospel without the threat of persecution or censure and would go home on Sunday. Suddenly I felt ashamed for my earlier thoughts, and I was grateful that I had only three nights in this room compared to Alexander's more than 8,000 in Castro's jail cells.

Then, as a balm for my weary soul, God sent a good friend to my room. She found me sitting in the middle of the soiled bed cover. While I attended my first meeting, she ran to a local supermarket, bought cleaning supplies, returned to my room, and had everything scrubbed spotless by the time I returned to my quarters. The room was still cramped, ugly, and had no hot tub, but it no longer mattered. The blessings of the weekend, the hearts touched, the lives changed took precedence over my discomfort. Laughter replaced my gloom, and love, joy, and peace filled my heart.

For a time I'd lost sight of my reason for being at the conference. During it I would meet a middle-aged woman who had been tempted to commit suicide less than a week before. I would speak with a young mother who couldn't see a loving God because of her weight problem. And a cancer victim would enrich my life with tales of praising her way through hair loss and chemotherapy.

For a few minutes I had lost my focus. But when I was ready to see the face of Jesus in my ministry once more, He was there, just as He promised. No games of hide-and-seek—just there by my side, renewing my strength and my joy.

And it reminded me of just how much God wants us to find Him, to see His many facets, to discover who He really is. That to know Him is to love Him. In the book of Revelation John described the angels that for 24 hours a day, seven days a week, continually circle the throne of God, praising Him.

When I first read about this class of angels, I thought, *How boring! While some angels do spiritual battle against demons and others go on rescue missions for God's clumsy kids, these poor angels just fly round and round God's throne and say, "Praise God."* Then one day an evangelist friend reminded me that on every lap the angels discover new and exciting aspects of His person and His character. And I began to understand what a privilege and honor it is for those praising angels. It was in praising that I began to see just how varied and beautiful God's character truly is.

First, knowing who I am and who He is elicits praise from my lips. I call this the perspective of praise. To understand my correct relationship to Him allows me the privilege of being His child. And I shake my head in wonder.

After all, I know who and what I am. I know all of Kay's dirty little secrets. Not only do I remember the sins of my youth, but also those pesky little peccadilloes I battle today. And I've learned that when I focus on the real me, I become discouraged and threaten to self-destruct. But also, should I compare myself with others—Betty's trouble with drinking, Elaine's rebellious children, Karen's perfect body—I feel either puffed up with pride or despondent with shame. The wrong focus spells trouble no matter how you look at it.

Seeking God through praise is like enjoying a kaleidoscope. When I was a kid I had one of those cardboard ones. You remember how those simple viewers worked with mirrors and broken glass? As you turned one end of the tube, the chips of glass shifted and new patterns emerged. It fascinated me for hours.

Somewhere along the way I lost the kaleidoscope. It wasn't until years later that I rediscovered their charm. In a little boutique along the California coast I found the most exquisite and unique kaleidoscopes I'd ever seen. Made of crystal and brass and costing many more dollars than I was willing to spend at that point in my life, I was captivated nonetheless. I fell in love with one brass kaleidoscope in particular. "What a lovely conversation piece this would make in the parlor," I reasoned as I lingered over the pricey bauble. While my heart said yes, my checkbook said no! My checkbook won the disagreement, with more than a gentle nudge from my husband.

My praise is like a kaleidoscope, though, showing me constantly changing views of my Father. Every view of Him is new, different, and beautiful. It's become an entirely new type of worship. I feel like I'm tasting a tidbit of the exhilaration the angels encircling His throne must experience as they discover new facets of their Creator.

One day a friend asked, "Why does God tell us to praise? Why does He need our praise?"

It wasn't until I explored my worship of praise that I realized that while God inhabits my praise and enjoys my praise, it is I who most need to praise.

God loves me so much that He's reached out to me in every way possible, through every metaphor and simile and illustration. He wants me to see and understand Him. And it has been through my praise that I've caught incredible insights into the God who calls Himself my Father. Who is this God I serve? What makes Him worthy of my praise? Twist the kaleidoscope tube with me and discover for yourself the multifaceted glory of our heavenly Father, our God and our King.

Ever-faithful Father

"You are My son; today I have become your Father."
—Psalm 2:7

"Catch me, Daddy, catch me!" The 5-year-old's eyes sparkled with eagerness as he perched on the ledge of the marble mantle piece, extending his arms toward his father. "Catch me!"

The father lifted his arms toward his son, "OK, jump! I'll catch you."

A grin flashed across the child's face as he thrust his body forward. Instantly, instead of reaching for his son, the father stepped back, allowing the child to crash to the marble hearth, bruising his knees and his heart.

The stern-faced dad lifted the crying boy to his feet. "There! Let this be a lesson. Never trust anyone, son, not even me. Don't ever forget that." And the boy didn't.

What a lesson to teach one's child! What kind of father would be so cruelly cynical? Is it any wonder that the boy would, when a man, have a difficult time grasping the concept of a loving Father-God?

A major greeting card company decided to offer free Mother's Day cards to the male inmates at a certain prison. Ninety percent of the prisoners took advantage of their offer. When Father's Day came around, the greeting card company repeated their generous offer. Out of 3,000 inmates housed in that facility, not one took advantage of it. Not only did the men reject the offer, but they did so with anger and violence. Even men who had had no contact with their biological dads had strong reactions to the thought of Father's Day. Those who minister to the prison population report incredible breakthroughs when a prisoner accepts God as his Father.

I called my father "Daddy." He was a quiet unassuming man who, if I had to choose one adjective to describe him, I would call faithful. He was a faithful provider both in financially good times and bad.

After Richard and I were married and teaching at Shenandoah Valley Academy, we had our first baby. In order for me to stay home with Rhonda, we chose to live on one check only, placing us on an extremely tight budget. Our main source of family entertainment during those years was fishing nickels out of our glass piggy bank to buy fudgsicles on our ride through the countryside. We came to the end of one extra-cold month and discovered that, because of the cost of heating fuel, we had no money coming in our check. Instead, we owed the school money for the privilege of working there. Newly married and fresh out of college, we'd never had the chance to build up a savings account for rainy days. So to us this was a deluge.

I was beside myself with worry. How would we live? How would we buy baby food for Rhonda? How would we buy groceries for us? feed the cat? (It would be decades before I discovered the secret of praising.)

As naturally as breathing, my thoughts turned to my dad. I hadn't a doubt but that he would find a way to bail us out. After Richard and I discussed the problem together, Richard agreed to call him. When he explained the situation to my dad, my father—not a man of great wealth—cautiously asked, "How much do you need?"

Richard hesitated. "Three hundred dollars should cover it." (Thirty years ago a family of three could live for a month on $300!)

My father heaved a sigh of relief. "Oh, is that all? I was afraid you might need several thousand, and I don't have that much on hand right now."

Not have that much on hand? His voice implied he would have given us, one way or another, several thousand if that's what we had needed. He offered the money straight out, a gift, no strings attached. Richard insisted it be a loan. My dad wisely acquiesced and assured Richard that there was no deadline for repayment. Three days later the check arrived in the mail as promised.

My marriage hadn't lessened my father's desire to provide for his younger daughter's needs. He could have told Richard, "I'm sorry to hear about your problems, but you two are adults now, married with a new baby. It's time you stand on your own two feet." But he didn't.

I've since learned that my Father-God never tells me to stand on my own two feet either. Quite the contrary, He's eager to meet my needs. One of His names, Jehovah-jireh, means "the Lord our provider."

The phrase appears in the story of Abraham and Isaac on the mountain. Abraham was ready to sacrifice his son as God had directed when the angel of the Lord stopped him and directed his eyes to a ram in the thicket (Gen. 22:13). The patriarch called the place Jehovah-jireh—"the Lord our provider."

God, my provider. That sounds like a daddy to me. Jesus said, "What father among you will give your son a stone when he asks for bread, or a serpent when he asks for a fish? If you then, being evil, know how to give good gifts to your children, how much more will the heavenly Father give the Holy Spirit to those who ask Him?" (see Matt. 7:9-11).

The Holy Spirit urges us to communicate with our Father. And it pleases God to hear from His kids, just as I, as a mom, long to hear from my daughters. I listen to their gripes and their woes, but I love it when they call just to say "I love you." That's praise.

Each of God's children has a life distinct from all others and an experience varying essentially from anyone else's. Any parent with more than one child will tell you how different each child is from the others. Nature, quirks, even choice of toys will vary among brothers or sisters. A loving parent accepts that child's love as it is delivered through that child's specialness, whether it be a plaster cast handprint, a cross-stitch wall hanging, a hand-carved breadboard, or a slobbery kiss.

"God desires that our praise shall ascend to Him, marked by our own individuality" (Ellen White, *The Desire of Ages*, p. 347). My own individuality? That can be pretty wild when you're talking about an aging "flower child" like me. No, I never actually lived in a commune or burned my bra, but I was born to be free. I struggled with the confines of society. One of my most freeing experiences came when I realized I was no longer restricted by the public's perception of what an English teacher should be— for I was a writer, and everyone knows how weird writers can be!

As a result, my preferences don't always resemble my sister's, whether biological or spiritual. And that's OK with God. He expects me to be an obedient child, not a cookie-cutter Christian, but unique in who I am.

A few years back Rhonda bought me an unusual basket for Mother's Day. The basket appears to be pine boughs, with needles attached, laced together with reeds and twigs. While packing it to mail, my new son-in-law, Tracy, looked at the strange, rustic bowl-shaped gift and wrinkled his nose. "Are you sure she's going to like this thing?"

"She'll love it," my daughter answered. And I did. My daughter knew me and my squirrelly tastes. Today the basket occupies an honored place on my living room bookcase.

In turn I allow for Rhonda's tastes that may differ from mine. And yes, she has her own style as well. So our Father takes delight in His daughters' specialness too.

Much of Jesus' ministry demonstrated the character of Jehovah-jireh, the Lord our provider. Remember Peter's frustration with the tax collector? "How will we pay our taxes?" the disciple worried.

I like Jesus' reply: "Go fishing." Fishing to Peter was the most natural thing to do. He'd cut his teeth on fishing lines, probably tying his first fisherman's knot before he could walk.

I see Peter as more than a little miffed at the cavalier way the Master appeared to dismiss his worry. Nothing is more insulting to a child than for a grown-up to make light of his concerns. Go fishing? "All right," Peter must have mumbled, "I'll go fishing!"

Imagine his surprise when the first fish caught on his hook also had a coin in its mouth—the exact amount needed for the tax bill. But if Peter had known his Master better, he would not have been surprised at all. God has a way of providing exactly what His children need when they need it. God is never too early and never too late, but always right on time.

Taxes—ever know anyone else who worried about how they'd pay their taxes? I have more than once, especially since I started my own business. Operating a small business requires that I file a special return more than 30 pages long! Along with the complicated forms, I am guaranteed, no matter how much I am allowed for my office and travel expenses, to have a sizable income tax bill. (Ah, for the days when we could expect to receive a chunky refund!)

So imagine Richard's and my surprise when we received a tax refund in the mail one day. We'd overpaid on our taxes! Impossible, but there it was. The refund check arrived two days before the spring on our garage door broke and we couldn't open the door to free our Chevy, our one and only means of transportation. Richard called someone to repair the door. It was 2:00 p.m. on Friday of Easter weekend. Most companies were closed for the holiday and would not reopen before Tuesday morning.

But the repairman came over within the hour, replaced the door spring, and handed us a bill for the same amount as our unexpected tax return.

That's the way God, our provider, works. I've seen it happen so many times. Our missionary daughter and son-in-law needed to raise several thousand dollars for their mission trip to Ireland the first summer of their ministry. On the Friday before they were to fly they had $700 in their account. By Monday noon they had the required $6,000, and they flew out of JFK International Airport with the rest of their team.

As Kelli and Mark's faith has grown, so have God's provisions. Again and again He has proved to be faithful. As with Peter, when problems surface the Saviour tacks a sign over the sweatshop of our religion, saying, "Gone fishing."

The root of this glorious liberty is in our daughtership (see John 1:12). The Spirit Himself bears witness that we are God's kids, and if His kids, then heirs to His wealth and privilege (Rom. 8:16-18). As a result we suffer with Him and we glorify with Him.

The entire human race is desperately religious. From the dawn of history not a man, woman, or child has been immune to the temptation to think that through our efforts we can change God. One way or another, whether by offering chicken sacrifices, gritting our moral teeth, or by not stepping on cracks in the sidewalk, we can soften the heart, and in some cases the head, of the Ruler of the universe.

We play our religious version of "Santa Claus Is Coming to Town." It's a dreadful Christmas song as well as a horrid reflection on our perception of God—making a list and checking it twice to find out who's naughty or nice. Peter's wringing of hands should have disqualified him for a miracle, right? Instead Jesus showed his disciple that He came to the world with no checklist or gradebook. He said, "I am your Messiah; I am your provider."

The heavenly Provider isn't out to save some tiny little sect of good boys and girls who have acquired a sufficient amount of "religious" money in their porcelain piggy banks. He opens His coffers to all His debt-ridden, overextended, deadbeat children in the world. Drying their tears and giving them a hug, He tells them, "Don't worry; I will provide. Just trust Me." Then He laughs and chucks them lovingly under the chin, adding, "Go fishing."

Eleven

And God Spoke

"You shaped me first inside, then out; you formed me in my mother's
womb. I thank you, High God—you're breathtaking! . . . I worship in ado-
ration—what a creation!"
—Psalm 139:13, 14, Message

D id you know that the letter combination "ough" can be pronounced nine different ways? A rough-coated, dough-faced, thoughtful ploughman strode through the streets of Scarborough, after falling into a slough, he coughed and hiccoughed.

Did you know that the verb "cleave" has two synonyms that are also antonyms of each other: adhere and separate?

Did you know that the word "checkmate" in chess comes from the Persian phrase *Sah mat,* which means "the king is defeated"?

And did you know that the name Pinocchio is Italian for "pine head"?

I love words. They fascinate me, entertain me, bring me delight, pique my curiosity, and titillate my imagination. My brain hears words in rhyme. I visualize them in my mind's eye, then mentally put them on the tip of my tongue and savor them like exotic-flavored jelly beans. Able to sniff out a good pun at 50 paces, I feel my ears tingle at the cadence of a good phrase. I chortle over silly songs and loony limericks and chuckle at misplaced modifiers and misapplied meanings. The well-phrased punch line of a joke sends me into a belly laugh. Words affect every facet of my life.

God is a Deity of words. Every thought, every creative impulse, and every human emotion must be expressed in a word before it can find life. Words are the basis of life. It wasn't until partially blind teacher Annie Sullivan gave blind and deaf Helen Keller the gift of words that the child could express the thoughts that had been circling aimlessly within her brain.

As a toddler, Helen suffered from an extremely high fever and as a result lost her sight and hearing. An extremely intelligent child, she existed as a raging animal trapped in the body of a child. One word—water—opened up the entire world to her. For instance, without a word the taste of a gumdrop was nothing more than a pleasant sensation on her tongue. She could not express such basic feelings as hunger, exhaustion, pain, or loneliness.

Helen loved ice cream, but she had no word for either the substance or the experience, hence she couldn't convey her delight at tasting the sweet confection or even understand why she enjoyed it. And she had no way to ask for more.

Words changed that. They gave her every experience of life. Once Helen discovered the magic of words, nothing could silence her. Thoughts and ideas flowed from her trained fingers on the wings of joy. She inhaled every new idea and concept as if she were the first to ever think such thoughts or experience such emotions. The ability to communicate re-created her.

Is it any wonder that the creation of everything began with a word? God spoke and things happened. Moses used the term Elohim in Genesis 1:26 for the God of Creation—the Father, Son, and Holy Spirit. In the New Testament John declared, "In the beginning was the Word, and the Word was with God, and the Word was God" (John 1:1). But let's go back to that first day when the glob of granite spinning about the sun was about to become a world. See Elohim gaze down at the useless water-covered rock and speak the words: "Let there be light" (Gen. 1:3, KJV).

Day after day the divine creative force spoke life into Project Earth. And day after day they declared good what they had created, including the crown of their creation—man and woman, made in God's own image.

Sometimes I catch a glimpse of myself in a mirror or plate glass window as I walk by and I think, *God's image? Hardly!* My spirits begin to sag along with the rest of my aging body parts. *Maybe if I . . .* and I begin to scheme ways to tone up this muscle or shed that cellulite. Perhaps I could spend more time at the gym on those exercise machines—you know, the ones that look like they've been restored from medieval torture chambers. Maybe then I'd begin to resemble the image of my Creator.

But alas, all the torture machines in the world, all the plastic surgeons' finely tuned talents, and all the artists at Revlon or Max Factor studios cannot erase the effects of thousands of years of sin. Even my personally sinful 50-plus years prevent me from being transformed into the image of Mother Eve.

Then I read in God's Word, "I AM THAT I AM" (Ex. 3:14, KJV). The God of Creation is the God of today. I'm not a surprise to Elohim or a disappointment. I'm just me—Kay Rizzo. And Elohim loves me. He said so in His Word. And you know His Word—it stands forever.

But if I worked out more to improve my mind, if I acquired advanced degrees, if I learned how to sing like Lucifer before the Fall, would it maybe make Elohim love me more?

The God of "I AM THAT I AM" can't love me or you any more than He does right now. He loves with an everlasting love. Time means nothing to the God of yesterday, today, and forever.

I was flying into Los Angeles at night and admiring the lights glittering below. *How beautiful,* I thought, *like diamonds, rubies, and emeralds on a blanket of black silk velvet.*

Then my practical side thought, *And beneath each of those sparkling lights are hearts that are broken. There are kids being abused. Murders, muggings, rape, violence of every kind.* My heart hardened at the reality. *Babies tossed into dumpsters by drug-ridden mothers.*

A perfectly formed baby thrown in a trash can—I couldn't imagine such a thing. I remember the days of pain and longing when Richard and I thought we'd never have babies of our own. With all the agencies to help, why would anyone throw away a baby? That happens in faraway places like Asia or Africa—right? Not here.

I thought of how God's heart must ache for each little one. Not quite the intention He had in mind for His newest creation. Mothers who do such things should be . . . I could think of several just punishments to inflict on such creatures. Then I thought of Elohim.

In my mind's eye I pictured God coming to earth especially for that one precious little bundle. "For God so loved . . ." Incredible. I saw Him reach down in my imagined dumpster and push a scrap of plastic away, toss aside a cereal box, then gently and lovingly lift the filthy, smelly, mewling body of that little child from the filth and coo in soft, loving tones, "You are so beautiful to Me . . . "

And as my eyes misted at this tender view of Elohim, a new thought hit me. *That same Elohim, that same Creator-God would do the same for the child's mother.*

"No!" I stared out the plane's window as we approached the airport for a landing. I didn't want to picture God tenderly lifting the drug-soaked, bug-infested, disease-ridden 16-year-old girl, mother to the discarded child, and singing gently to her, "You are so beautiful to Me . . ." How could that be possible? It boggles my mind. To say that God loves all His children of the world is easy. I picture clean, happy smiling faces of brown and yellow, black and white, not the blurry, listless eyes of this world's human garbage.

"But, Kay," God seemed to say, "I am the God of creation and re-creation. You see a girl who prostitutes herself for drugs while I see My little princess, and oh, how I love her. Your face may be cleaner than hers, but you still need to be cleansed by the blood of the cross. You need My re-creation balm to heal your wounds as well.

"I take delight in both of you. I exalt over you with love. I rejoice over you with shouts of joy [see Zeph. 3:17]. That's why I sent you to her. Who better can understand her pain and share the hope of salvation with her than someone who's already experienced the joy of that salvation?"

Another facet of the name Elohim comes from the word *alah*, which means "to declare, to speak." Scripture uses the name Elohim when speaking of God's covenants or promises with His people. God made a covenant with Noah in Genesis 6:18-22 that He would save Noah and his family. He promised that a flood would never again destroy the earth. He made a covenant with Abram in Genesis 17:7 and Jacob in Genesis 35:10-12. And each covenant Elohim made can be trusted, for He cannot lie. He cannot break His word, but is ever faithful.

In my search for the God of praise, I found one of His covenants that has become a favorite of mine in Psalm 103. Every time I read it, I discover new and exciting truths about the God of forever.

Psalm 103 is a hymn written as a Hebrew acrostic, celebrating the benefits of praising God and serving Him. David began and ended with "Praise the Lord, O my soul." Then he added, "All my inmost being." He understood the length and breadth of God's personal involvement with us. Here he shows God affirming the real David, the person He saw in David's mother's womb, the bombastic, strutting personality, the weird sense of humor, the tender heart, the person David was when he wrote the poem and the person he would become.

Every covenant has two facets. We see David's side of the promise when he praised God in his psalms, speaking from his innermost being. He praised God's holy name, telling God's people of the benefit that He bestows on them as their God. He showers all kinds of material and spiritual blessings upon them.

Take a moment and consider God's benefits to you. Where do you begin? From the turn of the gene pool to the talents you use every day; from the life-threatening diseases and accidents that didn't happen to the ones that did, from which you learned invaluable lessons about the Father; from the murky valleys of despair to the heady mountains of success—in everything, take a moment to remember His benefits.

Then David spells out God's side of the bargain. What do I receive when I praise? The first is forgiveness of sins. If anyone had sins, David did. From a twenty-first century perspective, King David did it all. He needed forgiveness. And so do I. Unforgiven sins hover over us like an umbrella, preventing God's blessings and His love from showering down on us. The sins of others against us do the same. We can be forgiven only in the same measure as we forgive. If I'm miserly in my forgiveness of my sister, I too will be forgiven grudgingly. But if my heart is open and effusive in my forgiveness, in like manner I will be forgiven.

We've all been there at one time or another, trapped in the war of the sisters (or brethren). You know how it goes. Mary said Ann's dress was too short. Susan heard her and reported it back to Ann, which made Ann retort, "She should talk. Her mascara looks like she applied it with a backhoe." And the war is on.

Within a few weeks everyone's taken sides. Families that once enjoyed each other's company now avoid each other. Children, once best friends, can't play together anymore. Oh, it might not be over a short skirt or makeup. In fact, it might be over something much more important, such as whose kid made the Christmas pageant while mine has to operate the curtains. Then again, it could involve who got elected head elder this year and who was ousted.

The results are the same. A rift begins tiny, then widens into the Grand Canyon of divorce. That's right—divorce. When God's family members, whether husband and wife, brother or sister, or just good buddies, forget to practice forgiveness, a divorce follows. And what began as hurt feelings develops into the "principle of the thing." Or as some might call it—pride.

How sad that we miss so many opportunities to become truly intimate with the Saviour. For Jesus is never closer to us than when we forgive or ask forgiveness. Forgiveness is the reason He came to earth and died for our sins. And yet we pull away, we shy from the spirit of forgiveness, all because of our own silly egos.

The disciples had been watching the Master. They observed Him slipping away in the early morning hours to be alone with His Father. Intently they listened to Him pray. Instictively they knew that His power came from this vital connection with His Father. And so they asked Him, "Teach us how to pray," meaning that they wanted the power that He received from His prayers.

I can picture Jesus looking at each of His beloved brothers, gazing deep into their souls. He could see their spirit of rivalry, their unbridled ambition, and the resentments built up from so many days and nights jostling for close proximity to the Saviour. And He knew what they needed most. Likewise He looked down through history at His motley, ragtag followers of each generation and knew what we would need as well—the spirit of forgiveness.

His prayer began with "Our Father."* Immediately He links us together, none better or worse, all the same—His kids. If my religion has no room for others, I cannot pray "Our Father." He is Father to the fatherless, a husband to the widow. God is above all and through all. "Behold what manner of love the Father has bestowed on us"; "Every good gift and every perfect gift . . . comes down from the Father" (1 John 3:1, NKJV; James 1:17, NKJV).

"Which art in heaven." Here we have the ID of the Father to whom we pray. People believed in many gods in Jesus' day, and they worship many gods today. Eastern religions have merged with what we call the New Age worship something that they call their father. But he is not the same. Thus God's kids identify their Father as the one living in heaven. It reminds me personally that my interests and pursuits must not be in earthly things, but in heaven itself.

"Hallowed be thy name." This is my praise. Praise is telling God how much you think He's worth. It establishes His authority over you. Jesus demonstrated the paradigm of praise in His prayer. Our prayers must begin and end with praise to the Father and not focus on ourselves.

His name is a strong tower to which we can run for protection (Prov. 18:10). Salvation exists in no other name (Acts 4:12).

"Thy kingdom come." Like the disciples, I have a rough time surrendering my sovereignty and accepting the righteous reign of God in my life. I choose daily to live in His kingdom.

"Thy will be done." Ouch! This one was difficult for the disciples. They didn't yet understand about surrendering their wills to the Father's. I find it equally as frustrating. Self-control? No, God control. Self-confidence? No, God confidence. Self-reliance? No, God reliance. "Whoever does the will of my Father in heaven is my brother and sister and mother" (Matt. 12:50).

I must forgive because it is God's will that I forgive. His will for me is no mystery. He wills that I bear no grudges, that I live in harmony with His other kids. It is His will that I study His Word and I give thanks in all things. "Your will, not mine."

"In earth, as it is in heaven." A perfect alignment of God's will. Jesus showed us the way when He said, "Not my will, but yours be done" (Luke 22:42).

"Give us this day our daily bread." Jesus wanted the disciples to know their one true source of everything. He desired that they realize that as God's children they have the right of prayer. Our petitions are important to Him. He promises to supply all our needs (Phil. 4:19). God is eager to bless His children.

I had a friend once who scoffed at the idea of thanking God for his food. "I worked for it," he said. "I earned every penny. I bought it from the grocer and carried it home." My friend missed the obvious—who endowed him with the strength to work, to hold down a job? Who gave the farmer the sunshine and rain to grow the wheat, or the baker the ability to bake the loaves, or the grocer the opportunity to stock his shelves?

When we pray "Give us this day our daily bread" we are also recognizing our responsibility to ease the hunger of others. As God supplies my needs, He enables me to show His love through my generosity. We need to ask ourselves, "If God's love were to be measured by my generosity, would the world see Him as a loving God?"

"Forgive us our debts, as we forgive our debtors." Ah, here we have the heart of the Saviour's prayer. Right up to His death on the cross Jesus lived this precept. We are forgiven as we forgive—an inescapable truism. Each of us must forgive and release our siblings from all resentment. Jesus the Shepherd became the lost sheep for our sake, becoming the model for our forgiving.

"Lead us not into temptation, but deliver us from evil." Life is a web of trials and temptations. But I have nothing to fear, for God will not lead me where His grace cannot keep me. However, if I deliberately choose to walk in the way of temptation, that is another matter. For example, if I am bothered with unclean thoughts, yet I surf the Internet for porno sites, I cannot expect God to cause my computer to crash. Or if I do constant battle with diet, I need to keep junk food out of my shopping cart. For when I deliberately choose to remain in a situation or I create a situation in which I am likely to be tempted, I defy my God to lead me not into temptation and deliver me from evil. I challenge Him, then, when I fall, rebuking Him for not keeping me as He has promised.

"Thine is the kingdom." Jesus' prayer begins and ends with praise. We affirm the fact that we are loyal subjects of God's kingdom.

"And the power." The disciples wanted power. It is what I crave as well. That's why when someone doesn't see life as I do, or discover the same spiritual insights at the same time as I do, or come to the same decision for their lives as I do, I resort to playing God. Wouldn't it be wonderful if every church installed a special bench outside the front door labeled "the judgment seat," reserved for anyone who dons the celestial robe of criticism or arrogance?

Yes, we should pray for power—not the power for convincing others of our intellect or theological positions, but God's creative power to turn darkness into light, fear into peace, and sorrow into joy.

"And the glory." The disciples, unlike us, of course, were seeking their own glory. As with 5-year-olds on the playground, their every action screamed, "Look at me! I'm the king of the mountain." We—oops, they—work to be seen and applauded by others. Unfortunately, glory is habit-forming. One can never get enough. Each taste makes us crave more.

One of the perks of praise is that it puts people, regardless of their rank, into proper perspective with the God of the universe. A view of God's glory sends the children of God to their knees. Any pride we might have had dissolves in the awe and magnitude of Elohim. And so we cry "Thine is the glory. You, Lord, and You alone."

"Forever." I cannot be anxious over tomorrow when I pray "forever." My God made a covenant with me. He said, "Never will I leave you; never will I forsake you."

Even the "amen" is part of my praise to God, because I am saying through it, "So let it be. Come what may, this is my prayer, Lord." "Amen" is our cry of triumph.

---

*This wording of the Lord's Prayer is from Matthew 6:9-13, King James Version.

Twelve

From Everlasting to Everlasting

"Praise the Lord . . . who . . . heals all your diseases . . . who redeems your life from the pit. . . . Praise the Lord, O my soul."
—Psalm 103:1-22

R ecently I heard a story about a woman named Ellen who tested positive for the HIV virus. Her unfaithful husband had exposed her to the disease. Anger seethed within her. She ordered him out of their home and out of her life. A trained nurse, Ellen knew the consequences of her disease.

"God, this isn't fair! I've been a good person," she argued in the night. "I've played by the rules, and this is what I get for it? If You're a just God, You have to heal me."

Ellen began to pray for her divine healing. She decided that along with her prayers she needed additional ammunition in her attack on God, the Healer, so she began to research God's Word for every reference to His promise to heal.

Eventually she discovered that the Old Testament name for God as our healer was Jehovah-rophe, or "the Lord, our healing." *Rophe* means health. She learned that Scripture used this name in the story in which God supplied His people with water in the desert.

In Exodus 15:22 God's people had been walking without water for three days, and He filled their needs. Jehovah-rophe turned the bitter waters of Marah sweet. As she read texts referring to God as healer Ellen listed them in her "Healing Notebook." Every day she added to her collection.

Ellen delighted in her discovery that in the New Testament God says He wants His people to walk in complete health. "I want that too, Lord," she reminded Him in her prayers. "You are the same yesterday, today, and forever, right? You healed lepers, the blind, even restored life to the dead. AIDS isn't a problem for You."

In her mind she relived Jesus' steps as He walked along the Sea of Galilee and as He entered towns where He healed all the sick brought to Him. She pictured herself inching to the front of the crowd and shyly asking to be healed. And oh, the smile He gave her. The thought warmed her heart.

During Ellen's study changes began to happen to her. She read the prophecy in Isaiah 61 about Jesus coming to "bind up the brokenhearted"—she was surely that—and to "proclaim freedom for the captives and release from darkness for the prisoners." Her life had never been so dark and so chained as it had been since she discovered her illness. She went on to read that He came to "comfort all who mourn." Ellen mourned the death of her marriage. But Jesus would "bestow on them . . . the oil of gladness instead of mourning." It had been so long since she'd laughed. "And a garment of praise instead of a spirit of despair."

Ellen said she laughed out loud at this one. A garment of praise? Her interest in what she wore had died the day her husband walked out the front door. She couldn't care less what she put on in the morning, or if she even bothered to get out of her nightgown. Everything seemed so empty and futile. Why care? *I'm going to die anyway,* she thought.

And here the Bible said Jesus came to replace her clothing of despair with a garment of praise. She'd barely finished reading the text when she tore off her scruffy pajamas, dug around in her dresser drawer until she found her prettiest undies, and took a steamy bubble bath, scented candles and all. Then she shaved her legs, dressed, and styled her hair. Hopping into her car, she drove to the mall to buy the brightest, prettiest, most impractical dress she could find, adding matching shoes and purse. On the way home she treated herself to lunch at a little neighborhood Chinese restaurant.

As she exited the restaurant, she had to make her way through a long line of people waiting to enter the shop next door. The sign on the plate-glass window read: "Free Clinic. Monday, Wednesday, and Friday. 1 p.m. to 5 p.m."

When she accidentally bumped against one grimy- and grouchy-looking man, he snarled, "Wait your turn, lady."

Disgusted, she answered. "I'm not going in there!" She turned to flee and ran into a white-haired woman. The woman gasped from the impact and staggered, then closed her eyes and slumped into Ellen's startled arms. Two young men waiting in line scooped up the woman and carried her into the clinic. Ellen followed.

The lack of proper equipment in the tiny clinic shocked her. A young doctor and a nurse's aide/receptionist staffed the place. Before she realized what was happening, Ellen found herself helping out. At closing time the doctor thanked her profusely and asked her if she could return the next day to help.

"You should know something about me," Ellen confided to the doctor. "I have been diagnosed with HIV."

The doctor smiled. "So have I. But you know what? These people are so grateful for our help. Almost everyone of them has a family member in the same boat, so they don't really care.

"When I got laid off from the hospital," he continued, "I thought my life was over. One of my former professors learned of my situation and raised the money so I could open this clinic. I don't have a budget to pay my staff . . ."

Ellen laughed. Her husband may have infected her with HIV, but he also kept her purse filled with plenty of cash.

Months passed with HIV medicine cocktails, doctor visits,

lab tests, and helping at the clinic. As Ellen continued her pursuit for spiritual healing, she no longer had time to mull over her misfortunes.

One Friday night Ellen felt more tired than usual and prepared for bed a little early. She'd barely turned back the bedcovers when the front doorbell rang. It was her ex-husband, Jeff. Clutching her robe about her slight body, she opened the door.

"Hi." He shot her a sheepish grin, taking in her mode of dress. "I hope I didn't waken you."

She sniffed his breath to determine whether or not he'd been drinking. He did that sometimes. "No, you didn't. What are you doing here?"

"May I come inside? I need to talk with you."

She hesitated a moment, then stepped back. "Only for a minute."

"It will only take a minute." He took a deep breath, biting his lip before he spoke. "How are you doing?"

"Fine."

"Your health OK?"

"Pretty much."

Jeff heaved a sigh of relief. "That's good. I've come to beg your forgiveness for my unfaithfulness." Her husband cleared his throat. "Can you ever forgive me?"

Ellen had dreamed of the day when she could spew forth all the poisonous venom fomenting in her mind. She opened her mouth to speak, but suddenly she couldn't remember all those practiced speeches she'd vowed that she'd make. As she looked into Jeff's eyes, she realized she no longer hated him. Somewhere along the way, she'd forgiven.

They went to the kitchen, where they sat at the table, sipping hot cocoa and talking into the night. Jeff told about going to a revival tent meeting and finding Christ. "One of the first steps the preacher said I needed to do was ask forgiveness for all the wrongs I'd done to others. And I thought of you first. I decided that if you could forgive me, maybe God could too."

God healed Ellen that night—not her body, but her soul. While she still carries the HIV virus, she knows she has been healed where it counts. She still must take her chemical cocktails around the clock. In addition, she still endures the lab tests and the medical visits. And the threat of AIDS remains a very real possibility.

From the first time she donned her garment of praise, Ellen began to heal. She believes that caring for others at the clinic facilitated her eventual healing. Gratefully she reports that Jeff cleaned up his life and keeps in touch.

As Ellen tells it, "a healing for my physical body is nowhere near as important as a healing for my spirit. I'm going to live in this shell only a few more years anyway, but God is preparing my spirit to live forever."

God could have opted to heal Ellen of HIV instantly, but He didn't. Instead He chose another method of healing, a healing she needed far more than she did from the virus. Jehovah-rophe, God our healer, continues to work in and through the lives of His people today.

Whether we call on El Shaddai (God most high) or Adonai (master or owner), or we celebrate Jehovah-nissi (the Lord our victor), or Jehovah-shalom (the Lord our peace) makes little difference. He is all these and more. Should we bow to Jehovah-tsabaoth (the Lord of hosts) or direct our worship toward Jehovah-tsidkenu (the Lord our righteousness), He is worthy of our praise.

It will be Jehovah-makkeh who will smite the evil one at the end of time. And spare the righteous.

Jehovah-gmolah will reward the faithful. As he rewarded the poor widow who fed Elijah, so Jehovah-gmolah honors our faithfulness (1 Kings 17:17-24).

And Jehovah-shammah is ever-present with His people. Psalm 18:11 promises that He is with us in darkness. Daniel 3:25

says He's with us through the fire. And Hebrews 13:5 tells that He remains with us through trials. He will never forsake us.

A friend of mine recently confided that he'd been experiencing panic attacks at night. The attacks seemed to stem from a fear that if he were to fall asleep he would die. He would drop asleep for a short time, then jerk awake in panic, feeling pain around his heart and a racing heartbeat.

It went on for months with my friend never getting more than an hour or two of sleep. Soon it began to affect his eating and his disposition. Finally in desperation he talked with a physician friend about his own age. What a relief it was for my friend to learn that such attacks were common among men going through their mid-life crisis. When asked if there was any medication for it, the physician picked up his prescription pad and wrote, "Recite Psalm 23 while falling to sleep." My friend took the doctor's advice, and the attacks lessened until one morning he realized he hadn't had a panic attack in months; his appetite had returned, and he no longer behaved like a bear roused during hibernation.

Millions of people over the years have found the doctor's prescription for peace effective. I had never thought of the six short verses of the chapter to be words of praise. While they do not once use the term *praise,* they are praise indeed, for they allude to eight redemptive names for God.

"The Lord is my shepherd."* Christ is Jehovah-rohi.

"I shall not want." Jehovah-jireh supplies all our needs according to His riches (Phil. 4:19).

"He makes me to lie down in green pastures; He leads me beside the still waters." God is our Jehovah-shalom, our God of peace.

"He restores my soul." Jehovah-rophe took our infirmities and our sickness and by His stripes healed us.

"He leads me in the paths of righteousness." Jehovah-tsidkenu's righteousness, not ours, brings our salvation.

He leads me "through the valley of the shadow of death."

Jehovah-shamman will never forsake us. No matter how dark the valley may become or how deep the shadows, they are only shadows, shadows of the death Jesus has already suffered for us.

He prepares "a table before me in the presence of my enemies." Jehovah-nissi always triumphs. We are more than conquerors in His victory.

"And I will dwell in the house of the Lord forever." My life on earth might be brief, but I have an eternal lease on a corner room with a view in the palace of my heavenly Father—Elohim, the I AM THAT I AM.

Got a reason to celebrate? Got a reason to love Him? Got a reason to praise His holy name? I know I've caught but a tiny flash, a glimpse of the incredible being He truly is.

It kind of reminds me of the time Richard and I were standing at Crown Point overlooking the Columbia River Gorge in Oregon, watching a big orange sun sink below the horizon. Suddenly, without warning or fanfare, I spotted "the green flash" for but an instant. I couldn't believe my eyes. I'd seen a rare and remarkable occurrence.

For those of you not familiar with the green flash, it's a natural phenomenon that happens at sunset when just the right refraction of the atmosphere occurs. Whether he was blinking or looking away at the precise moment it occurred, my poor scientific husband missed it.

The green flash is truly rare, but the insights into our God are just waiting for us to turn to Him, to shed our myopia and tilt our faces upward in praise. I don't want to miss one flash of His presence.

---

*Wording of Psalm 23 is from the New King James Version.

Thirteen

Interactive Praise

Just call me grandma. I love it. My grandson Jarod is the most gifted, most advanced, most athletic, most intellectual, has the best sense of humor, best nature—and the list goes on and on and on. And every grandma I meet says the same things about her grandchildren. If we take these observations at face value, then the next generation will be one sensational group of individuals! As I patiently listen to their bragging, I think, *Yes, of course, but you haven't met my Jarod yet.*

After Jarod's birth he and his parents lived with us for several months. I had the pleasure of watching that perfect little body develop from an almost inanimate form (except at 2:00 a.m.) through the smile and roll-over stages.

Kelli traveled with her musical group throughout her pregnancy, singing the same songs each evening. During labor and delivery Mark played one of the Celebrant Singers' CDs. When colic started or when Baby Jarod had trouble sleeping, Kelli played the Celebrant CD, and he would fall asleep in no time.

When he would be upset or fussy, I would take him out to my garden swing—my prayer swing—where we would swing and I would sing "The Boat on Galilee." Even when Jarod reached the wiggly stage, during which he hated to stay in one place, a ride on my swing to the tune of "Rock, rock, rock, little boat on the sparkling sea," and he would lean his head against my chest and quietly listen.

When Jarod turned 6 months old Kelli and Mark rejoined their team for a mission trip to Slovenia and Croatia, and I wept a few tears. I wondered if Jarod would even remember me when he returned home at the end of the summer. He was so young.

The day I got the call that they were back in town and they asked me to come down to the Wal-Mart parking lot to meet them, my fears became a reality. The infant had become a baby, and that baby wasn't any too sure who this strange woman was. He let me hold him, since he was used to strange people taking him from time to time, but to voice his disapproval, he turned his face away from me. When I would adjust him in my arms, he turned the opposite way. My chirpy little coos could not convince him I was someone he knew.

Jarod's suspicions continued until I took him out onto the prayer swing. As I set the swing in motion, he squirmed as if he wanted to be put down. But when I began to sing the familiar song, he stopped wiggling, leaned back his head on my chest, and listened.

When I considered Jarod's reaction to the children's song, I thought of how parenthood (and grandparenthood) can give us a taste of what God is like. Then I recalled Zephaniah 3:17: "The Lord your God is with you, he is mighty to save. He will take great delight in you, he will quiet you with his love, he will rejoice over you with singing."

The *New American Standard Bible* put it like this: "The Lord your God is in your midst, a victorious warrior. He will exult over you with joy, He will be quiet in His love, He will rejoice over you with shouts of joy."

My favorite version of this text appears in *The Living Bible.* "'For the Lord your God has arrived to live among you. He is a mighty Savior. He will give you victory. He will rejoice over you in great gladness; he will love you and not accuse you.' Is that a joyous choir I hear? No, it is the Lord himself exulting over you in happy song."

If I were to paraphrase the text, it would go like this: "Your heavenly Father is with you always. He's an Olympic gold medalist in every event, a champion to the max. When He thinks of you, He shouts and boasts to the universe, 'See My kid? Isn't she incredible?' At other times He becomes quiet as He reflects on His deep affection for you. He celebrates who you are with joyful singing."

Jarod will be returning to our home after a mission tour of Cuba. By then he'll be walking and running instead of crawling. Before he gets here, I'll take the time to babyproof the house. I'll need to secure the cupboards and move my "pretties" to higher ground, but do you know what? I don't care. I can hardly wait. Having him home again will be worth it all. Even now I wonder if Jarod will remember the swing and our song. Somehow I think he will.

When I first discovered the marvelous concept of praise, I, like a child, focused on its power—what praise could do for me and how I could use it to better my life. At the same time I researched the precept of praise, it's definition and purpose in God's plan. It was beautiful, incredibly beautiful. It wasn't until my praise began to mature beyond infancy that I experienced interactive praise.

I wonder if God passionately anticipates my special times with Him. Yes, passionate, for as I type these words, tears well up in my eyes at the thought of Jarod's return. I have to pause long enough to grab a Kleenex tissue from the box and blow my nose.

Some theologians are uncomfortable attributing human emotions to the Supreme Being. The ancient Greeks thought God must be little more than a stature without any feelings, and many

Christians, including the great Reformers Luther and Calvin, took similar positions. After all, they assumed, God has to be above emotion. He is a perfect Being, and by their definition, to have feelings would cause Him to change, and something perfect cannot change or it will become imperfect. But that is not the kind of God the Bible reveals.

Zephaniah 3:17 reveals the passionate side of our Father. When I was a child our church had a woman who never smiled. She never smiled at church, at baby showers, at wedding receptions, or even at church parties. She was a grouch. As an adult I now wonder if perhaps she didn't feel well, had arthritis, or maybe even had had a stroke and couldn't smile. I don't know. But as a child I steered clear of her because she seemed so cross. My friends did the same thing. She was one scary person.

If my God acted anything thing like that woman, I wouldn't want Him in my midst! He'd be peering over my shoulder, checking out my every move. However, I've discovered that whenever I invite my God to my "party," my party gets nothing but better.

He showed His joy at the wedding feast, doing whatever it took to spare the bride's family any embarrassment for running out of wine. At the supper in the upper room He sang with His friends. Recently I saw a video on the life of Christ, and at the wedding feast the director had the actor portraying Jesus dancing with the other men in a traditional Jewish dance. That's my God. That's the kind of Jesus I love and serve, one full of compassion and love, but also filled with joy.

In John 15:11 He says He told us these things "that your joy may be full" (KJV). And in John 17:13 He prays that His kids will have a "full measure" of heaven's joy. Joy implies passion—not a placid waving of one's hands in blessing, but exuberant celebration. When I think of God's grace for me, I want to shout and sing and dance with joy.

God exults over us in festive pleasure and with great delight.

He is ecstatically happy. In the parable of the lost coin (Luke 15:8-10) He urges, "Come and share in my celebration." Our Lord wants us to participate in His joy, His celebration. Jeremiah 31:20 asks, "Is not Ephraim my dear son, the child in whom I delight?" Here we see delight again—leaping and shouting for joy.

The same word found in Zephaniah 3:17 describing God's pleasure over us appears in verse 14 to depict our rejoicing over Him. Scripture exhorts us to sing. After all, God sings over us. We delight in God. He delights in us. Back and forth, God and His people enjoy one another—interactive worship.

At Creation, when God looked over each day's accomplishments, I cannot picture Him solemnly saying "It is good" in a monotone voice. He created the heavens and the earth for His pleasure and His joy. In my sanctified imagination, I see the divine Triumvirate standing on a hilltop surveying the results of their labors and bursting into laughter and song.

How does God react when He thinks of you? When I ask teenagers this question, some wrinkle their noses; others say "Yuck!" But the truth is God neither grimaces or frowns. He celebrates. As one Christian writer put it, "He explodes in glad celebration—in divine glee."

Exaggeration? Hardly. Delight in Hebrew means "leaping for joy." First Kings 1:40 records that after David killed the Philistine the people followed after him, playing flutes and rejoicing greatly (the same terms as in Zephaniah 3:17) "so that the ground shook with the sound."

A story on the Internet tells about a small boy taking his grandmother to a ball game. When a player hit the winning run, the boy screamed and yelled while the grandmother sat stone-faced. Seeing her lack of response, the boy shouted in his grandmother's good ear, "It's OK to be happy, Grandma; we're not in church."

If God uses such words to describe His joy toward us, can we not respond with a similar unbridled glee, a raucous mirth—all part of the Hebrew definition? Sound a little irreverent, too rowdy for your liking? Stay tuned for the rest of Zephaniah 3:17, again from the NASB:

"The Lord your God is in your midst—" Right now! Where I am today. As the psalmist wrote, God "inhabitest the praises" of His people (Ps. 22:3, KJV). His presence, passion, and joy surround me.

"A victorious warrior." He's won all there is to win. And He did so at Calvary. It's time His kids break out the band, beating those drums, crashing those cymbals, blowing those trumpets, and shaking those tambourines. We're home free because He paid the price. I can't sit still. I must rejoice. He too rejoices.

"He will exult over you with joy." Here's where the interactive praise comes in. In your own private worship, have you ever experienced joy to the extreme? I've made horrendous mistakes in my life of the most mortifying kind. And when I think of the extent of God's forgiveness, I am moved to tears, then to joy, because my sins are gone! And they can be dug up from the depths of the sea only by a scuba-diving devil—if I let him. How can I help but sing? If all this celebrating and noise bothers you, you will especially appreciate the next phrase of the verse.

"He will be quiet in His love." My older daughter is a quieter cut of the family fabric. Once she confessed to me that I—exuberantly sanguine Kay—exhaust her at times. And it's true. My enthusiasm can be boundless—until I hit an invisible point, then boom, my energy level plummets and all I want to do is curl up with a soft pillow and a good book. So for all those of quieter bent, and that includes all of us at one time or another, God promises that He not only exults over us in "festive pleasure," but He will be "quiet" over us in His love.

Talk about a deep abiding love, one that is so profound it leaves the God of the universe speechless. He is moved to complete silence.

Have you ever been left speechless? I have, believe it or not. On Richard's and my twenty-fifth anniversary Kelli and Rhonda took us out to eat at a Mexican restaurant to celebrate. While there they talked about a party they'd considered throwing for us on our special day.

We assured them that just being with them was enough. Then Rhonda pushed a brochure across the table and said, "Thought you might want to read up on London. You'll be going there during Christmas break. Happy Anniversary!"

Both Richard and I—neither of whom are ever at a loss for words—stared at her in stunned silence. "How? Where?" we stammered. We knew they didn't have any money. Kelli was still in college and Rhonda had just graduated.

The girls laughed, then told us they'd solicited money from all the family across the U.S. to help send us. Again we were stunned into silence. What a surprising act of love.

God so "loved the world" that it made Him speechless. He couldn't find the words to tell us how much He loved us, so He died for us. And we continue to cause Him to be speechless at times. In our interactive worship He holds us quietly in His arms and enjoys our presence.

Sometimes when I hug Richard, there is no need for words. My silence isn't a threat to him. He understands. As one Christian writer put it, "God's silence is not a reflection of disinterest, but enjoyment. God is sincerely captivated by you and words would only spoil it" (Sam Storms, "God's Passionate Love," *Spirit Led Woman* August/September 1998, p. 45).

The Living Bible paraphrase of Zephaniah 3:17 adds "and not accuse you." When we come to Him to worship, we can safely rest in His arms without fear of rejection, correction, or censure. The Holy Spirit will reprove and instruct in His time. And that time is not when we are resting in the Father's arms.

The Living Bible has paraphrased the rest of the text in this way: "Is that a joyous choir I hear? No, it is the Lord Himself exulting over you in happy song." Not in a funeral dirge, nor in a "he did me wrong" song, but the God of the universe exults over you in happy song.

I like happy songs. Hardly a moment goes by that I'm not humming some ditty. Several years back musician Bobby McFerrin wrote and recorded "Don't Worry, Be Happy." And once the catchy tune got into my head, I couldn't get it out. I found myself humming it wherever I went. As much as I liked the rhythm and upbeat philosophy, I assumed that a serious-minded Christian could hardly take the message to heart—that is, until I discovered the joy of praise and the beauty of interactive worship. Then "Don't worry; be happy in Jesus" became a way of life.

Imagine the unformed, uninhabited spheres way out there in the farthest corners of the universe, floating through space in utter silence, when suddenly, the Creator bursts into song over one of His kids and the music reverberates through space. Perhaps the song is militant in His praise, perhaps He sings a song of laughter and rejoicing, or perhaps He chooses a gentle lullaby, but suddenly His love speeds through space on the wings of a song, shattering the interstellar silence, pouring light into the darkest black hole, sprinkling life on the floating shards of cosmic dust, bringing comfort and divine approval to my heart.

When I was a teenager my father's praise was important to me. He was a man of few words. I remember coming downstairs from my room one day to model my new gown I'd bought for a banquet at my high school. Daddy smiled. I could see the pride in his eyes. He said, "Honey, you look purty in your new dress." I had my father's approval. I could safely attend the event that alternately frightened and fascinated me. His words comforted his awkward teenage daughter. And his smile gave me confidence.

My heavenly Father's eyes sparkle with pride as well when I enter His presence wearing my garment of praise (Isa. 61:10). And I can almost hear Him say, "Honey, you look purty."

"Don't worry; be happy!" His joy and acceptance of me allows me to worship with the Father in total abandon and joy. I cry with Him over my sins. I agonize with Him as I contemplate the cross. I rejoice over His victory and over my victories.

Halel, the Hebrew word for praise, means intense worship. This is the gift He holds out to me and to you. He offers to enter into a worship with His kids that is so intimate, so complete, that words cannot express His deep, abiding love, and yet so incredible that He and I burst into song and shout and, yes, leap for joy. It removes my spiritual myopia so that I can see the boundless glory of who He really is.

Fourteen

To the Heart
of My Worship

"Let him kiss me with the kisses of his mouth—for your love is more delightful than wine. . . . We rejoice and delight in you; we will praise your love more than wine."
—*Song of Solomon 1:2-4*

R ecently the San Juaquin Valley gained a new radio station, one that plays "golden oldies." "Kisses Sweeter Than Wine" is one of those favorites I love to hear. I listen to the station when riding in the car. Let one of my old favorites come on the radio and I find myself submerged in memories of days long gone. My husband says that when this happens, I get a quirky grin on my face and a distant look in my eye. The song takes me back to an earlier, more innocent time, an era of matching sweater sets, of bouncy pony tails and shiny penny loafers.

When I first heard "Kisses Sweeter Than Wine" I didn't recognize the source of the phrase. Who would have thought some composer would be quoting Scripture in a 1950s pop song? Of course, Shakespeare, another man of many words, had a habit of doing the same, as have many authors since.

The phrase "kisses sweeter than wine" comes from a book in the Bible that is an enigma to many theologians. In English it has become known as the Song of Solomon. In the original Hebrew, hence the Latin and Greek versions, its title is the Song of Songs, expressed in the superlative as the Best of Songs.

Tradition attributes the writing of the book to wise King Solomon. Others believe it might have been written later and dedicated to the beloved king.

To many scholars it is simply a love poem, erotic in nature. Some believe it to be a pastoral poem put to music and sung at religious festivals. Others point to it as a drama, a primitive play, if you will. And still other scholars regard it as a stream of consciousness piece—some man's inner thoughts strung together.

Early Christian scholars, influenced by Greek philosophy, interpreted it as an allegory of the passionate love God has for His bride—the church.

I'm not a scholar, but I like the idea of a divine allegory. It's consistent with the character of the God I've come to know and love. The same God has used every metaphor possible to express His love to His people. His word pictures invoke imagery that speaks to the potter, the shepherd, the son, the father, the husband, the brother, the farmer, and the merchant. He says "I love you" in a thousand ways. And so to have Him speak to me as a lover is not a stretch for me.

It disturbs some biblical scholars that the Song of Songs does not mention God or contain such words as "sacrifice," "temple," "priests," "prophets," or of religion in general. That's not an accident as far as I'm concerned.

Falling in love with Jesus must be simple and pure, uncluttered by human theology. A pastor friend of mine once said, "Correct theology is important only as it directly relates to my relationship with Jesus Christ."

I like that. I think of it this way. I take a brick of vanilla ice cream and turn it out onto a silver tray, then I begin adding all kinds of good things—chocolate syrup, butterscotch syrup, marshmallows, nuts, candy sprinkles—and your mouth begins to water. Then I throw on a spritz of taco sauce (good stuff), a dollop of soy sauce (mmm), olives, mustard, onions, grated cheese—and motor oil for good measure. It keeps my car running smoothly, doesn't it? When I do this in children's church, my audience erupts in protest. By the time I finish my nauseating ice-cream sundae, you can't even see the vanilla ice cream. Then I invite someone from the audience to come up and taste and see that my sundae is good. Usually no one is willing.

Except that one day Dena took me up on my offer. She took one of my spoons and pushed the goop aside, then, using a clean spoon, she scooped up some of the clean vanilla ice cream and ate it.

Ah, my point exactly. When the psalmist told me to "taste and see that the Lord is good," he was talking about the pure and lovely Jesus, not all the human theological additives. Getting to know Him first, falling in love with the real Jesus, I am then prepared to discern what theology goes with the Jesus I love and what it doesn't. Our love gives me new insight when I read the Scriptures.

The Song of Songs is that kind of book. No jargon, no "sauce," gets in the way of a pure love story. As I read it for myself I discovered that it also describes my interactive worship.

First, let's review the story so skillfully woven into the poetry. A pastor friend of mine, Mike Leno, describes it something like this: "Once upon a time . . ." A young girl, her skin bronzed from working in the sun, unlike the other girls in her community with their alabaster complexions, has brothers who mock her for her tanned skin and her washboard flat, undeveloped figure.

Someone announces that the young king is coming to town to look for a woman to become his queen, and all the unmarried girls are aflutter, hoping to become that chosen one. When our young girl's brothers catch her preparing for the king's visit, they laugh and mock her for her dark skin and for her flat chest and undeveloped form.

The king visits the town and leaves without choosing a queen from the fair maidens. The next scene shows our young girl working in the fields, perhaps at the town well filling her water pouch, when she meets a handsome young stranger, a shepherd. By accident and then by design, they meet at the well each day and soon become acquainted, then fall in love.

One day she goes to meet him at the well, and her shepherd isn't there. That day, the next, and the next, he doesn't return. Brokenhearted, she barely notices when the announcement goes out to the community that the king is returning to the village in search of his queen. When her brothers tease her, she ignores their barbs. Her shepherd, her friend, is gone—nothing else matters. She also doesn't notice that time has taken care of her body. It has softened and rounded in all the right places.

On the day of the king's visit her family drags her to town. The other girls vie to be in the front row so that the king will see them and choose them. The king arrives in a flurry of horses, soldiers, and banners. Everyone kneels before him. His carriage stops in front of where our young girl's family is bowing. He steps down out of the royal carriage, walks to our young girl, and extends his hand to her. She lifts her eyes in surprise to discover that it is the king who is her friend, her beloved.

And as in good fairy-tale fashion, she is swept away by the king and they live in wedded bliss for all time. That the king posed as a shepherd in order to find the woman who would love him for himself and not for his wealth or his title only adds magic to the story.

Regardless of whether or not you read such a tale into the words of Song of Songs, our nameless young woman enjoys three relationships with the man who would become her lover.

First, she knew him as her king. And she worshiped him in the manner proper to his position. I worship my God as my king. My praise of who He is as my Creator and my king reflects that worship. In His presence, I can see how good He is and how bad I am. And I fall in awe at His feet. "Majesty, worship His majesty . . ."

But as in the story, He doesn't leave me worshiping at His feet. The second element in the story is friendship. The communication between two friends is deeper than the relationship between a monarch and his subject. Just as the young king wanted his bride to love him for himself and not for his position, so Jesus desires to have a closer relationship with me. He longs for me to be His friend.

He takes me to green pastures and to clear pools of water. We share our laughter and our tears. Jesus reveals His heart to me, and I do the same with Him. He is "closer than a brother."

But the story doesn't end with a "good buddy" friendship, as rewarding as that may be. The friendship that budded on the grassy hills outside the young girl's town, that grew to love beneath the hot Mediterranean sun, brings the shepherd/king back to his beloved. He takes her by the hand and unfurls a magnificent banner declaring his love for her. Imagine how pleased our young bride was when she read his declaration of love emblazoned on the banner waving in the breeze. Claiming her as his bride, he takes her to his palace for the most glorious banquet he can provide.

God wants to be my beloved. He vows to be my lover 24 hours a day, seven days a week, and 365 days a year for the rest of eternity. "Never will I leave you; never will I forsake you!"

My husband and I vowed "till death do us part." But God's marriage vow to me goes beyond eternity.

A bride doesn't celebrate her marriage to a man because he healed her or saved her or set her free from bondage—she extols their union because I am his and he is mine.

When I come to my Bridegroom with no requests for a new dress or a new chariot, with no complaints about the garbage disposal acting up or the outrageous phone bill, I experience a deeper attitude of worship and praise than I ever could when He was only my king or my friend. I worship Him with the highest form of praise.

In Song of Songs 2:8-10 the young woman thrills at the voice of her beloved. When Richard and I were dating he could phone me and make my day. And when he would come calling at my dormitory, I would skip down the stairs two at a time to greet him.

The beloved says in Song of Songs 4:9, 10, "You have ravished my heart, my sister, my spouse; you have ravished my heart with one look of your eyes. . . . How fair is your love" (NKJV).

God wants nothing less when I worship Him. My Beloved wants me to thrill at the sound of His voice, to burst into smiles at the sight of Him, and to tremble at the touch of His hand. I know, as a bride of 35 years, that my husband still likes to hear me say, "I love you." So God longs to hear our declarations of love. I don't need to be a Shakespearean actor to speak to Him. He wants to hear your voice expressing your love for Him. God's heart is drawn individually to you.

Occasionally when Richard and I were dating I baked him batches of chocolate-chip cookies. I made the cookies because I knew he liked them. But he didn't marry me because of my ability to make the best chocolate-chip cookies in the world. If that were what he was looking for, he would have made Mrs. Fields his Mrs. Rizzo. No, for some reason I still can't explain, Richard's heart was drawn to Kay Hancock, the squirrely kid from Troy, New York.

In the same way, God didn't go looking for the best chocolate-chip cookie baker or the best gospel singer or the "hostess with the mostest" when He searched for me. He came for me because I can love Him in a way that no one else ever created can love Him. My love is as individual as my thumbprint or the arrangement of freckles spread across my nose. Our experiences are uniquely ours.

And I've only just begun to explore the depth of His love. I remember when, before Richard and I were married, I would tell my mom how much I loved my young Italiano, and she would smile and say, "Honey, you are just beginning. You have no idea how great it will become." She was right. Don't let anyone fool you, regardless of how Hollywood might portray the magic of young love.

It can't hold a roomful of perfumed candles to old love.

Outrageous worship? You bet. Who wants a lukewarm love that dissipates with the dawn? Discover for yourself how the imagery of the Song of Songs enriches your worship. He will anoint your love with the incense of heaven. In the process you will discover how to love Him more fully.

I am sure the young bride of our story continued to respect and worship her king. And she kept on enjoying the companionship of her best friend, but nothing in their previous relationships could ever measure up to her relationship with her beloved.

Before Christ returns for His bride, He will have a people who will worship Him fully. When the Samaritan woman by the well tried to distract the Master from His mission by bringing up age-old arguments about the where and how of worship, Jesus zeroed in with, "My people will worship me in spirit and in truth."

Talk about outrageous worship, passionate worship, a complete, interactive worship with the God of the universe, a worship that won't end in death, but will live forever. Passion begets passion. Our passion for our Saviour will give us a passion for His people.

Go ahead. Fall in love. Take the risk. Let the words to the greatest of love songs guide you into a new intimacy with your Creator. And you will taste and see how good our God really is. When you strip away the garbage and the gook that stands between you and the pure love of Jesus Christ, you will enjoy Him more than you ever imagined possible. Your passion will permeate everything you do. And you will see your Saviour as He truly is.

"O come, let us adore Him, O come, let us adore Him, O come, let us adore Him, Christ, the Lord. For He alone is worthy, for He alone is worthy, for He alone is worthy, Christ, the Lord."